FROM DIEPPE TO D-DAY

The Memoirs of Vice Admiral 'Jock' Hughes-Hallett

FROM DIEPPE TO D-DAY

THE MEMOIRS OF VICE ADMIRAL 'JOCK' HUGHES-HALLETT

Introduced by
Allen Packwood BA, MPhil (Cantab), FRHistS, OBE

rf

FRONTLINE
BOOKS

FROM DIEPPE TO D-DAY
The Memoirs of Vice Admiral 'Jock' Hughes-Hallett

First published in Great Britain in 2023 by Frontline Books,
an imprint of Pen & Sword Books Ltd, Yorkshire - Philadelphia

ISBN: 9 781 39904 557 5

Typeset in Chennai, India
by Lapiz Digital Services.

Printed and bound by CPI UK

Pen & Sword Books Ltd incorporates the imprints of Pen & Sword Archaeology,
Air World Books, Atlas, Aviation, Battleground, Discovery, Family History,
History, Maritime, Military, Naval, Politics, Social History, Transport, True Crime,
Claymore Press, Frontline Books, Praetorian Press, Seaforth Publishing and
White Owl

For a complete list of Pen & Sword titles please contact:

PEN & SWORD BOOKS LTD
47 Church Street, Barnsley, South Yorkshire, S70 2AS, UK.
E-mail: enquiries@pen-and-sword.co.uk
Website: www.pen-and-sword.co.uk

Or

PEN AND SWORD BOOKS,
1950 Lawrence Road, Havertown, PA 19083, USA
E-mail: Uspen-and-sword@casematepublishers.com
Website: www.penandswordbooks.com

CONTENTS

PREFACE

13 November 1954

Sir,

Following your retirement from the Active List of the Royal Navy, my Lords Commissioners of the Admiralty desire me to convey to you an expression of their appreciation of your distinguished services over a period of 39 years.

My Lords recall that you entered the Royal Navy on 15th September, 1915, and, as a junior officer, combined exceptional technical knowledge with administrative ability and practical efficiency of a high order. During your early career you displayed particular zeal, ability and ingenuity and on three occasions earned My Lords' appreciation for work in connection with the development of torpedoes and on other occasions for specially good work in ships in which you served.

After promotion to Captain on 30th June, 1940, until December, 1941, you served as Deputy Director of Local Defence at the Admiralty, where your scientific knowledge was of particular value, and from December, 1941, until October, 1942, you were Naval Adviser on Combined Operations. In the *London Gazette* of 11th March, 1941, you were Mentioned in Dispatches for zeal, resource and devotion to duty.

In your next appointment from October, 1942, until November, 1943, you performed very valuable service as Senior Officer Force J and additional Chief of Staff to the Commander-in-Chief, Portsmouth. You were responsible for the planning of the St. Nazaire raid and commanded with gallantry, daring and skill the 252 ships and craft in the Dieppe raid, in recognition of which you were appointed a Companion of the Distinguished Service Order in the *London Gazette* of 2nd October, 1942.

During this appointment you also played a leading part in laying the foundations of the plan for building up and training the British and United States assault divisions in this country; you formulated the basic naval plan for the invasion of Europe which was approved by the Combined Chiefs of Staff. Subsequently you developed Force J into a pattern for other similar assault forces. In carrying out all these varied and valuable duties you displayed singleness of purpose and conspicuous ability, combined with great strength of character.

From December, 1943, until February, 1945, you commanded H.M.S. *Jamaica* and in the *London Gazette* of 6th January, 1944, you were again Mentioned in Despatches for your gallantry, determination and skill throughout the action in which the German battleship *Scharnhorst* was sunk.

It was a source of great satisfaction to My Lords when, in the *London Gazette* of 4th September, 1945, you were appointed a Companion of the Most Honourable Order of the Bath in recognition of your distinguished services in "Operation Overlord" and as Commanding Officer, H.M.S. *Jamaica*.

After serving as Captain of H.M.S. *Vernon* from June, 1946 until May, 1948, and in command of H.M.S. *Illustrious* from June, 1948, until June, 1949, you were promoted to Rear Admiral on 7th January, 1950. After a short appointment connected with the control of civilian employees in Fleet Establishments, you were appointed to the Admiralty as Vice Controller and Director of Naval Equipment, in June, 1950. During the two years of that appointment, you continued to display that originality of mind and outlook for which you had become well known in the Service.

During your next appointment as Flag Officer, Heavy Squadron, Home Fleet, from July, 1952, until December, 1953, you were promoted to Vice Admiral on 2nd February, 1953, and in your final appointment on the Active List before you asked to retire on 8th September, 1954, you were engaged for nine months on important work with the Committee concerned with the comprehensive review of Officer Structure and Training in the Royal Navy.

I am, Sir,
Your Obedient Servant,
J.S. Lang

INTRODUCTION

The memoir you are about to read is held by the Churchill Archives Centre at Churchill College, Cambridge, where it has sat since 1990 in three folders in a single acid-free box. What we know is that the 246 pages of annotated typescript were produced by Vice Admiral Hughes-Hallett as part of his projected and never completed autobiography, provisionally entitled *Before I Forget*. His nephew Richard, who ultimately inherited and deposited the manuscript, was confident that his uncle – or strictly half uncle – must have written it in the late 1960s, after his retirement as the Conservative MP for East Croydon, but before a severe stroke in late 1970 and his death in 1972. Interestingly, there is another fuller version held by Library and Archives Canada, while related correspondence and papers can be found in London's Imperial War Museum.

What survives in the Churchill Archives are two chapters on 'Combined Operations' and 'Force J', along with a separate detailed typescript on 'The Dieppe Raid'. This material has been kept together as a record of Hughes-Hallett's time as Naval Adviser on Combined Operations (December 1941 – October 1942) and subsequently as Senior Officer Force J (October 1942 – November 1943). This was a key period during which he was charged with developing, testing, commanding and training the personnel, mechanisms and tactics needed to develop an amphibious offensive capacity and take the fight across the Channel onto enemy-occupied shores.

The preface to this volume, a 1954 Admiralty document issued on Hughes-Hallett's retirement from the Active List, summarises his career and achievements. It stands on its own, so that there is no need to repeat the detail here, but it makes clear that he entered the Second World War as a highly regarded officer, making captain in June 1940 at the age of 39. He was clearly considered something of a scientific specialist, and his role as Deputy Director of Local Defence at the Admiralty, and knowledge of 'anti-invasion measures' led naturally to his selection by Mountbatten for Combined Operations.

It was a trust that was reciprocated, and Hughes-Hallett's text reveals his deep admiration and loyalty to his patron.

What follows is a fascinating first-hand account of how Combined Operations developed. The text plunges the reader back into the complexity and uncertainty of the time, giving a picture of the competing and ever-shifting demands of war; highlighting the bureaucracies and inter service rivalries that had to be negotiated and reminding us of operations that were contemplated and did not happen, such as plans to seize or raid the Cherbourg Peninsula in France or Alderney in the Channel Islands. All of which ate up limited time and resources.

We accompany Hughes-Hallett as he tries, but fails, to observe the St. Nazaire raid from one of the bombers during a thunderstorm, as he undertakes assault training for Dieppe with Canadian troops and as he commands the naval force during the ensuing raid itself (thereby giving him a unique vantage point as both a planner and a commander to talk about the myriad reasons for its failure).

There are wonderful vignettes of key personalities, such as Field Marshal Smuts, Mountbatten and General Montgomery, who offers Hughes-Hallett one key piece of advice for command in battle; namely that the 'strength of mind required is simply to do nothing and refrain from dithering'.

Ultimately, it is a story about the challenges, successes and setbacks involved in scaling up operations; from Captain March-Phillips tiny small boat commando raids, to the successful attack on the dry dock at St. Nazaire in March 1942, through to the much larger and unsuccessful operation against Dieppe in August, and on to the creation of a permanent assault force (Force J), which would ultimately provide the basis for the D-Day landings (although by June 1944 Hughes-Hallett was commanding the cruiser HMS *Jamaica*).

As such, it illuminates an important transition period from the offensive to the defensive, placing the successes and failures in their broader context, and showing how Allied grand strategy was translated into practical delivery.

Allen Packwood BA, MPhil (Cantab), FRHistS, OBE

ABBREVIATIONS

A.A.	Anti-Aircraft
A.C.2	Aircraftman 2nd Class
A.C.O.	Allied Command Operations
A.O.C.	Air Officer Commanding
C.-in-C.	Commander-in-Chief
C.G.S.	Chief of the General Staff
C.M.S.F.	Co-ordinator of Ministerial and Service Facilities
C.O.	Commanding Officer
C.O.H.Q.	Combined Operations Headquarters
C.O.S.	Chief of Staff
C.O.S.S.A.C.	Chief of Staff to the Supreme Allied Commander
D.S.C.	Distinguished Service Cross
F.J.I.s	Force J Fighting Instructions
F.O.P.S.	Future Operational Planning Section
G.I.C.N.A.F.	General Instructions for the Conduct of Naval Assault Forces
H.M.S.	His Majesty's Ship
H.Q.	Headquarters
I.R.A.	Irish Republican Army
L.C.A.	Landing Craft, Assault
L.C.F.	Landing Craft, Flak
L.C.I.(L)	Landing Craft, Infantry (Large)
L.C.I.(S)	Landing Craft, Infantry (Small)
L.C.P.	Landing Craft, Personnel

L.C.S.(S)	Landing Craft, Support (Small)
L.C.T.	Landing Craft, Tank
L.S.I.	Landing Ship, Infantry
M.G.B.	Motor Gun Boat
M.L.	Motor Launch
M.T.B.	Motor Torpedo Boat
N.C.O.	Non-Commissioned Officer
R.A.F.	Royal Air Force
R.A.N.	Royal Australian Navy
R.N.	Royal Navy
R.N.V.R.	Royal Naval Volunteer Reserve
S.P.	Self-propelled
S.P.A.	Self-propelled Artillery
S.S.R.F.	Small Scale Raiding Force
U.S.	United States
U.S.A.A.F.	United States Army Air Force
U.S.N.	United States Navy
V.C.	Victoria Cross
V.I.P.	Very Important Person
W.R.N.S.	Women's Royal Naval Service

Chapter 1

COMBINED OPERATIONS HEADQUARTERS

In October 1941, Captain Lord Louis Mountbatten, as he then was (later the Earl Mountbatten of Burma, K.G., G.C.B., etc.) was appointed Adviser on Combined Operations, in the rank of Commodore 1st Class. My own appointment to Combined Operations Headquarters (C.O.H.Q.) as his "Naval Adviser" came during December 1941. I learned afterwards that Mountbatten had asked for me because of my previous association with anti-invasion measures. There was also a "Military Adviser" in the person of Brigadier Charles Haydon, who also commanded the Special Service Brigade, which was the collective title given to the Commandos. Group Captain Willetts of the R.A.F. was appointed as the "Air Adviser".

In practice the position of the three Advisers was quite different on account of the differing organisation of the three Services. Thus, the Group Captain was primarily a liaison officer with the R.A.F.'s functional Commanders-in-Chief, while Charles Haydon was a fairly independent provider of raiding troops. My own function was chiefly that of making outline plans for raids in consultation with the other advisers and keeping both the Admiralty and the Joint Planning Committee informed of what was in our minds at C.O.H.Q.

When first appointed I had still not shaken off an attack of jaundice and was obliged to work only short hours until after the turn of the year. However, I was able to go with Mountbatten to Camberley on 13 December 1941, to attend a rather grandiose tactical exercise (without troops) organised by General Alan Brooke (later Field Marshal Lord Alanbrooke), the Commander-in-Chief, Home Forces. He had obtained from C.O.H.Q. a forecast of the landing craft that would be available in July 1942, and hence the total "lift" that would be possible

1

for a cross-Channel operation in the coming summer. He therefore instructed each of the Home Army commanders to prepare and present an outline plan for the seizure of the Cherbourg Peninsula, for holding it for a week, and for the subsequent withdrawal to England.

With the predictable exception of General Montgomery (South Eastern Command), each General allowed his C.G.S. to present his Army's plan. Monty came last, and, after explaining the hazard of such an operation, went on to point out that it would be both easier and more worthwhile not to withdraw the troops but flood the Carentan Marshes and hold the peninsula. This exercise was repeated a month later at St. Paul's School, and Monty confirmed his previous conclusion. This created a powerful impression on my mind and was destined to have an important effect on our fortunes two months later.

Before relinquishing my Admiralty appointment, I had, on my own initiative, made a small start with our own invasion preparations! There was at that time no adequate Operational Plotting Room for the Naval Commander-in-Chief at Portsmouth, and this was now urgently needed as part of the Radar Coastal Plotting Organisation. Admiral Sir William James, who was then Commander-in-Chief, Portsmouth, suggested an underground operational headquarters tunnelled into the chalk of Portsdown Hill, just below Port Southwick.

Convinced as I was that, when it became our turn to invade, our main landings would have to be in the central Channel, I suggested to Admiral James that we might make his underground operational headquarters large enough for a joint Service Staff, and well enough equipped to direct the launching of an invasion fleet. Admiral James was enthusiastic, and the project went forward with hardly a word to anyone.

Nevertheless, my chief impression from our experience of anti-invasion planning in 1940 and 1941 was the enormous magnitude of the problems to be overcome before even a minor amphibious operation could be mounted and successfully carried out in home waters within range of the two chief metropolitan air forces, coupled with the truly immense difficulties of anything approaching an overseas invasion. In this respect I was at odds with the prevailing military thought. Few Army officers showed any understanding of the magnitude of the problems to be overcome before a big amphibious operation could be mounted and carried out: few, that is to say until they were personally involved. The same applies to some military historians – notably Liddell Hart in his *Military History of the Second World War*.

Yet, if the war in Western Europe was ever to be won, the re-conquest of France was generally agreed to be an inevitable prelude.

North-west France was the obvious battle ground for several reasons. Whether we liked it or not, we had to maintain continuous fighter supremacy over the south-east of England to protect ourselves from German bombers, and we had to maintain a large army in the United Kingdom to protect ourselves from invasion.

In consequence, the principle of economy of force dictated that we should be able to use the fighters and the troops based in the United Kingdom for the dual purpose of defence and counterattack. Furthermore, the United Kingdom was the easiest place in which to assemble and supply the great American army which would be needed for an invasion, and a new front in France would threaten the Achilles heel of Germany, namely the Ruhr. Against this the mounting of a cross-Channel invasion offered no prospect of strategical or tactical surprise, or even, so we thought at first, of technical surprise. Furthermore, the changeable weather and the strong tidal streams in the Eastern Channel offered as big a threat to small and slow-moving landing craft as did the Germans themselves.

There had been a certain amount of study of amphibious operations between the wars, but only on a microscopic scale, and with only medium raids as the ultimate goal. Certain techniques had come to be accepted: notably that the troops must be landed in specially designed landing craft, self-propelled and protected against small arms fire, so that infantry could be put ashore at first light to secure a beachhead, on which tanks could be landed as it grew light.

Nevertheless, the principal conclusion of the "Combined Operations Handbook" produced between the wars was that an opposed invasion would not be practical in modern warfare. Why then should we bother? Partly because we had no choice, and partly because an exaggerated importance was attached to the development of "helm-free" gunnery.

The aversion to amphibious operations which coloured inter-war thinking was largely based on our failure at Gallipoli, and this, in turn, was ascribed chiefly to the inability of warships to take on shore batteries, except when such batteries are visible to the gun-layer or director-layer of the warship. Normally, however, it is possible to site Coast Defence Batteries so that bombarding warships will be obliged to fire "blind" – that is to say the guns will be laid on an artificial horizon and pointed by means of a plotting device. Observers ashore, or from the air, will report the fall of each salvo to the bombarding ship to enable spotting corrections to be made. With the apparatus available during the First World War this procedure could only be carried out if each bombarding ship maintained a steady course at low speed, or, better still, was at anchor. In either case she became a sitting duck to the gunners ashore.

During the 1930s there had been a drive to improve the Royal Navy's fire control equipment, as a result of which heavy ships could bombard without restrictions on their course or speed. It was widely believed that as a result of this "helm-free" gunnery, warships would have the measure of shore batteries, thus making combined operations more attractive than they had been in 1915. Experience in the Second World War showed this to be so, but the balance between attack and defence was not changed as much as had been hoped, for the simple reason that coast defence batteries played a relatively less important part.

The threat of aerial bombing and the need for aerial supremacy had become the decisive factors by 1940. Indeed, the only place where the coast defence batteries were established on a truly great scale was the area between Calais and Boulogne. It is said that vessels at sea off Dover were exposed to the fire by over 100 guns of 30cm calibre and above. Yet all these guns were unable to stop the days of systematic mine-sweeping by three ocean-going mine-sweeping flotillas in mid-Channel during Operation *Starkey* in September 1943. No minesweeper was sunk and only one naval rating was killed. Radar jamming and modern smoke-making methods did more to redress the balance against warships than did "helm-free" gunnery. This example is only worth mentioning because it illustrates how misleading forecasts can be when they are based upon the technical development untested by actual experience in war.

The need to develop forces for amphibious operations was, as might be expected, obvious to Mr Churchill from the day of the Fall of France. He appointed General Bourne, the Adjutant General of the Royal Marines, as "Director of Combined Operations" and no time was lost in setting up C.O.H.Q. The Adjutant General is now called the Commandant General, and is in fact the head of the Royal Marines. It is therefore strange that General Bourne never suggested that Royal Marines were the ideal raw material out of which to form the Commandos. But his interest lay in creating a Royal Marine Division of which the War Office disapproved, and kept it from operating, by denying it a "tail".

However, General Bourne was also overanxious to carry out tiny raids, chiefly, I suppose, on account of their stimulating effect on morale. Nevertheless, these operations achieved nothing, and a number of very gallant young officers, such as Commander Congreve, lost their lives to little avail.

In July 1940, Mr Churchill superseded General Bourne by Admiral of the Fleet Sir Roger Keyes, afterwards Lord Keyes. At the same time, he gave instructions that raiding forces of up to 10,000 men should be organised and trained, and that a matching number of tank and infantry landing craft should be constructed. He also claims in Volume II of his books on the Second World War that as that as far back as 1917 he had suggested the construction of an artificial harbour for a particular operation. Unfortunately, his paper was not only never published, but was never circulated to those responsible in the Second World War, which might have spared us a great deal of anxiety later on.

So far as I can make out, the vision of C.O.H.Q. during the Keyes "Regime" never went much beyond a bigger and better Zeebrugge-type raid. Moreover, the Admiral and many of the older officers at C.O.H.Q. had great difficulty in grasping the need for close co-ordination between all three Services.

The Admiral's patience became exhausted, and he developed a strong preference for raids on Norway. These chiefly involved co-operation with the Naval Commander-in-Chief of the Home Fleet, which he understood. It was largely the friction that developed between Keyes and the senior officers in the R.A.F. and the Army that led to his replacement by Mountbatten, but in any case, Mr Churchill's own ideas far outran those of the Admiral.

Yet even Churchill underestimated the scale of what would be required. For example, in July 1940 he urged the construction of landing craft for 600–700 vehicles to match the 10,000 troops, but the actual ratio demanded by the Army at that time was one vehicle for every three soldiers.

In October 1941, C.O.H.Q. was in a somewhat confused state. It was in part an Operational Headquarters responsible for planning and mounting raiding operations in home waters; in part it was also a Government Department in miniature concerned with the provision of special craft and special weapons, as well as acting as a training authority for the personnel required for such operations. No clear distinction had, however, been drawn between these functions, and the suitability of many retired senior officers, for the purpose of their widely varied duties, varied greatly depending upon their background and previous service.

As A.C.O., Mountbatten inherited not only C.O.H.Q., but also the so-called "Combined Operations Command", which included specially fitted troop-carrying ships, the Special Service Brigade, and a number of raiding craft to ferry troops or tanks from the sea-going ships to the shore. It also comprised a number of training bases mostly situated in the Inverary area on the western coast of Scotland.

Very soon after joining C.O.H.Q., I began to doubt the wisdom of having a Combined Operation Command because it imposed a vast amount of administrative work and strain on Mountbatten himself, and diverted his time and thought from operational policy and plans. Nevertheless, he had from the outset taken a great step forward by separating the operational and planning part of the work from the administrative, technical and training side.

This separation was of crucial importance, as also was a certain tidying-up of the Administrative Organisation by separating training from the maintenance of material, and the procurement of new types of Landing Craft. Rear Admiral Horan, who had served at C.O.H.Q. under Admiral Keyes, remained on as head of the administrative side of our affairs. Even so, the organisation was far from perfect, and Mountbatten in particular was grossly overloaded with work. Yet he made an even greater contribution than getting C.O.H.Q. more soundly organised. His boundless energy and enthusiasm infused a new spirit. In particular, the operational planning side knew for the first time that their work was real and earnest; that the raids they were working on would in all probability be carried out.

When I first joined it was assumed that the main British effort, at least for the coming six months, would have to be confined to raids – chiefly cross-Channel – but also against Norway and possibly on the French Atlantic coast. At that time there was no firm directive governing the planning and mounting of raids, any more than it was conceded that C.O.H.Q. should have the exclusive right to do this work.

On the contrary, the Home Force Military Command advanced the extraordinary view that the English South Coast and the French North Coast should be likened to a front line of two armies locked in trench warfare, with the Channel as the no man's land between them.

From this it was argued that the initiative for mounting raids should rest with the Army Commanders, whose areas faced a particular piece of enemy coast. No raids took place under this arrangement, if only because all the specialist craft needed to carry raiding troops came under C.O.H.Q., which alone possessed the requisite three Service Staff to ensure close liaison with the R.A.F. and Naval Commanders-in-Chief. It was therefore tactically agreed that Mountbatten should be the authority for mounting raids, although this was not embodied in a formal Directive until early in March 1942, when General Paget at length agreed that all future raids should be under the auspices of C.O.H.Q.

Going back to December 1941, when I joined, each of the "Advisers" had already been provided with a small staff. The proliferation of Staff Officers at C.O.H.Q., which was much criticised at the time, came later, after two or three successful raids had made many officers keen to jump on this new bandwagon.

How far such criticisms were justified is a matter of opinion on which it would be rash to dogmatise. I am one of those people who believe that all Service Staffs at Whitehall – particularly the Army Staffs – grew to a monstrous size during the Second World War and have remained grossly inflated ever since. But C.O.H.Q. was in no way exceptional, although it was more noticeable because it was new. Whether all the work done at C.O.H.Q. was essential, or whether some of it could – or should – have been done away from Headquarters is, again, a matter of opinion, but all the officers who flocked to Mountbatten's banner were certainly kept extremely busy. C.O.H.Q., nevertheless, was like all other headquarters in one respect, most of its vital output was the work of a comparative handful of officers who served there. The same applies, and has no doubt always applied, to the Civil Ministries.

But to return to C.O.H.Q. at the end of 1941, on the naval side, I had at first only two Staff Officers; Commander David Luce (afterwards Sir David Luce, G.C.B.), and Lieutenant Commander Costabadie: both were officers of outstanding ability, and both were destined to die before their time, though not before Sir David Luce had held Office as First Sea Lord. A little earlier Commander Michael Hodges joined as a Communications Specialist and head of a Combined Communications Staff with the title of "Chief Signal Officer Combined Operations". Sub-Lieutenant Ranald Boyle, R.N.V.R. was later appointed as my personal assistant.

By the end of 1941 the officers in charge at the Combined Training Centre at Inverary had become pretty set in their thinking about technique to be followed for embarking troops in landing craft, for the run-in of the Landing Craft to the beaches; for clearing the landing craft of troops after they had beached; and for the subsequent return of the craft to their parent ships. As a newcomer, I felt no inclination to suggest changes, which would have been resented by the retired senior officers who had done a wonderful job in training the Landing Craft crews. Nevertheless, as the officer who was to become responsible for planning cross-Channel raids, there were two points upon which I felt obliged to intervene.

The first concerned distance from the shore at which landing craft should be lowered. The practice at this time was to aim at about 4 miles. On a clear night the coastline should be both visible and identifiable from the bridge of an Assault Ship at this distance. Each flotilla officer could therefore be given an accurate bearing on which to run in. To aid the landing craft in keeping on this bearing various types of infra-red beams and beacons had been developed and installed in the assault ships, one idea being to keep a beam trained on the beach so that the guide of the landing craft need only keep in this beam which was visible through special binoculars.

I felt strongly that it would be rash to assume that German coastal radar in the Channel area was markedly inferior to our own. This meant that the Assault Ships must stop and lower their landing craft at least 10–12 miles offshore. This meant in turn that a flotilla of L.C.A. would take between two to three hours after being lowered to form up and run-in to the beach.

During such a time they might be carried anything up to 6 miles or more by the tidal streams and their position could in any case be based on no more than their Parents Ship's dead reckoning at the point of lowering. The chance of an Assault Ship obtaining an observed position was slight at such a distance from the shore. In other words, the decision to keep the L.S.I.s so far offshore involved a fundamental change in the navigational problems facing the Landing Craft. I do not think any of us fully realised this at the time and it was not until just before the raid on Dieppe that we decided to introduce a new functionary, whom we called the "Local Naval Commander", at each landing area or beach.

This officer, usually an experienced Royal Naval Lieutenant Commander, crossed the Channel in the ship carrying the Senior Officer of a group of assault ships. The Army officer commanding the troops embarked in the same group, was with him in the same ship. They therefore got the most up-to-date-information available to the Senior Officer when the ships stopped to lower their craft. At this stage both the Local Naval Commander and the officer Commanding the troops transferred to a motor launch fitted with special navigational aids which acted as a guide to all the L.C.A. Flotillas of a group of Assault Ships. Only when very close to the beach did the Army Commander transfer from the navigational M.L. to an L.C.A.

This arrangement ensured a continuity of Naval Command and liaison with the troops that had been lacking before, but which became essential with very long runs-in to the beach.

Whether we need have kept the Assault Ships so far offshore remains a moot point to this day. Certainly, right up to the end of the war the technical performance of German Radar lagged far behind that of our own, as also did the ability of the Germans to make effective use of such Radar information as was available to them. But when one is at war with a great and modern nation like Germany, noted for its industrial and technical achievements, it is dangerous to assume that any lead one may have in one particular field at a given moment will be maintained for very long. At any rate our policy achieved its object, because I know of no case in which British Assault Ships were detected from the shore before their landing craft had got well clear of them.

My other concern was with the size and performance of the Landing Craft which had been developed. The L.C.A. had gradually been evolved as a result of practical experience and had much to be said for it. It was popular with the troops, who felt secure behind the protection of its bullet-proof plating. Its load of twenty-five infantry was well suited to the assault phase of a wide variety of minor operations, and its small size enabled young officers to become efficient Commanding Officers after relatively short training.

On the other hand, its slow speed and dependence on very calm weather rendered it unsuitable for cross-Channel raids, unless it could be carried close to its objective in an Assault Ship, though for the reasons given in the preceding paragraph, the advent of Radar had made this a less attractive proposition. In some ways the Higgins type of "Eureka" boat, also designed for twenty-five soldiers, and afterwards called the L.C.P., was more suitable for the Channel raids. Indeed, they were often called "raiding craft". They were much better sea boats and twice as fast as "L.C.A.", but they had wooden hulls and were driven by petrol, and offered no protection to the soldiers from rifle and machine gun fire.

I felt strongly that for Channel operations we needed a number of "Giant Eurekas" capable of crossing the Channel under their own power in average weather at a speed of at least 15 knots and carrying about 100 soldiers – all under cover – all behind and below bullet-proof plating. This involved a craft nearer in size to a standard coastal craft, that is to say an M.L. or an M.G.B. I reached this conclusion after a day spent with Commander Cook, R.A.N. in February 1942. At that time, he was commanding the raiding craft base and was about to act as Naval Commander for the raid on Bruneval.

I next put the proposition to Mr A.J. Merrington, the Naval Constructor attached to C.O.H.Q. As a result of our talk, Merrington and Tom Hussey evolved what was later called the "Landing Craft Infantry (Small)" – (L.C.I.(S)) – of which only fifty were built, ten being armed to act as support craft. These craft did not become operational until the summer of 1943; too late for raiding – as the raiding season was by then over. Like so many British designs they were a little bit too "Rolls-Royce". They carried 120 troops at a maximum speed of 17–18 knots and were completely encased in bullet-proof plating. Their engines were petrol driven and their 8,000 gallons of petrol was carried in two large tanks in a compartment kept filled with carbon-dioxide.

This proved to be a more effective fire precaution than might have been expected. I remember on one occasion a rocket from a rocket craft fell short and burst after hitting an L.C.I.(S) on her upper deck over the engine room only a few inches from the bulkhead which separated the engine room from the fuel tanks. Each of these rockets carried about the same charge of high explosive as that in an 8" projectile. One man in the engine room was killed, a rent was torn in the upper deck, and the bulkhead leading to the fuel tanks was ruptured, but there was no fire.

During Operation *Overlord* in 1944, the British L.C.I.(S) played a notable part, albeit on a smaller scale than the American designed L.C.I.(L), which was a much larger, but less sophisticated, version of the L.C.I.(S). In particular, in the fierce battle for Walcheren Island, the attacking troops were carried in L.C.I.(S) and supported by the support version, the L.C.S.(S). Although they suffered heavy losses, the island, deemed by some to be impregnable, was captured.

Our most urgent task was to select suitable targets for raids on France and Norway. Everyone agreed that in the first instance it must fall to the Navy to suggest objectives since it was no use suggesting places which could not be reached by the appropriate landing craft or other vessels.

One raid on Vågsøy (Norway) had already been carried out. It had been planned, but in outline only, in Sir Roger Keyes's time, largely, I fancy by Charles Haydon and David Luce, and was executed with great skill and success. But there were no other ready-made plans, although planning for a parachute raid on a Radar Station at Bruneval near Le Havre was well under way. Accordingly on 21 January, David Luce, Costabadie and I, sat down to make tentative proposals for one raid every month up to and including August. We were not so much concerned at this stage with the intrinsic value of objectives on a particular raid, but rather with the feasibility of reaching the place undetected.

We soon concluded that Norway was not so attractive as we had at first assumed on account of the distances being so great and the weather too unpredictable. We therefore concentrated our attention on the Channel area, bearing in mind that the parachute raid on Bruneval was timed for 27 or 28 February.

Our first choice, (for early March) was a house on the Ostend seafront which the Germans were using as a rehabilitation centre for Luftwaffe pilots who had recovered from wounds. For the end of March, we suggested a raid on St. Nazaire to be followed a few days later with one on Bayonne. For May we proposed an attack on Alderney; the island to be held for as long as practicable providing the raiding force was able to occupy it completely and quickly. By the occupation of Alderney, we hoped it would at least be possible to cut the German coastal route to the Atlantic ports by which they had sustained much of the U-boat campaign since the French railway system was reported to be inadequate to keep the U-boats supplied.

For June we chose Dieppe, as by that time we expected to have sufficient landing craft to lift an entire division. For July we felt that a repeat raid on Dieppe would achieve surprise and lead to the slaughter of specialist German engineers likely to be at work repairing and strengthening the fortifications. Finally, for August we visualised a landing on the south bank of the Somme, to seize a beach through which a large force of armoured cars could pass and make a dash towards Paris.

All these were quickly agreed, and the following day the broad pattern had also been agreed by Charles Haydon and Group Captain Willetts, and we had already initiated a study of the detailed intelligence reports of each place. On 23 January I disclosed my ideas to Mountbatten, who agreed in principle, and asked for outline plans to be prepared and discussed with him as soon as possible.

Chapter 2

THE GREATEST
RAID – ST NAZAIRE

I will now digress to write in greater detail about the St. Nazaire raid, because the events which preceded it were symbolic of what was destined to happen so often later in the war.

It has frequently been asserted that St. Nazaire was chosen because of its great dock – the only place where the *Tirpitz* could be docked on the Atlantic coast. In fact, this is not so. We first chose St. Nazaire because we wanted to surprise the Germans by one of two raids on the Atlantic coast. St. Nazaire happened to be the most distant objective which could be reached by a raiding force with only one daylight period on the voyage. We thought that with luck and careful timing, the force might get there unobserved, and this indeed happened. Two daylight periods, we felt, would be tempting providence too far, and therefore although a raid on Bayonne near the Spanish border had many attractions, we felt it wise to time it for a few days after St. Nazaire.

St. Nazaire also attracted us because although one of the most heavily defended ports in Europe, a glance at the chart revealed a fatal defect in the siting of the defending batteries. The main approach channel ran close inshore for some miles and was covered by several heavy coast defence batteries. To the seaward, there was a great area of shoal water which dried out at low water to form huge mud flats. However, the range of the tide is very great and we thought it possible that there would be enough water the flats for vessels drawing not more than 12 feet "at extraordinary spring tides", that is to say twice a year.

If this was so, it would be possible for the raiders to pass over the shoal water and enter the deep-water channel very close to St. Nazaire itself, and run the gauntlet of only one of the batteries. Consultation with the "Superintendent of Tides" at the Admiralty (a delightful title), confirmed that this was so, and he advised that the end of March would be the ideal date in 1942.

After selecting these possible objectives, the next step was to study the detailed intelligence and ask for scale models to be made.

C.O.H.Q. had its own Intelligence Officer in the person of the Marquis of Casa Maury, who in private life had been the manager of the Curzon Cinema who had held a temporary Commission as a Wing Commander in the R.A.F. Of all of those serving at C.O.H.Q he came in for most criticism from the Admiralty and the War Office; not so much on personal grounds, but rather because the Naval and Military Intelligence Staffs strongly objected to having an intermediary between themselves and C.O.H.Q. His function in fact was not so much the collection of Intelligence as the collation and presentation of the three dossiers prepared by the three Service Departments. This task he performed with astonishing despatch, displaying considerable skill, artistry and imagination.

Looking back, I have no doubt that he saved our Operational Staff a great deal of time and I am sure that Mountbatten was quite right to insist upon having his own intelligence officer as a link between C.O.H.Q. and the Service Departments. Furthermore, Casa Maury was not inhibited from seeking information from any source which he thought might be able to supply it, whether that source was in uniform or a civilian. For example, he discovered that the lock gates at St. Nazaire had been designed by a British engineer subsequently employed by the Southern Railway Company and responsible for the gates at the great dock at Southampton.

As soon as I mentioned St. Nazaire to Casa Maury, he told me that about a year before, the Admiralty had invited Sir Roger Keyes to plan an attack with the object of putting its great lock out of action. Detailed intelligence had been assembled and was available, together with a large-scale model. The project had, however, been judged too hazardous to proceed with. David Luce and I once advanced the destruction of the lock as the prime object of the proposed raid, thereby ensuring the enthusiastic support of the Admiralty. The original outline plan took only about an hour to evolve and was as follows: An "expendable" ship drawing not more than 12' of water should be obtained and should embark one complete Commando. She should sail from Plymouth or Falmouth accompanied by four Fairmile motor launches, one motor torpedo boat, and one motor gun boat fitted with special navigational aids. The route to be followed, and the timing, should be laid down with precision after consultation with the Admiralty Superintendent of

Tides and the Naval Commander-in-Chief, Plymouth, who was known to have made a detailed study of the timing and routing of the routine German Meteorological flights.

After passing over the flats, and once past the coast defence battery, the expendable ship should increase speed to about 20 knots and ram the outer lock gate. The Commando, the ship's company, and the demolition parties would disembark over the fo'c'sle on to the lock gate and take cover behind two long air raid shelters which the Germans had built along both sides of the dock. A charge of 8 tons of high explosive should be built into the expendable ship somewhere below her bridge, at the point where experts calculated would be abreast the lock gate by the time the ship had come to rest.

After the men had taken cover, the big charge should be exploded, thus demolishing the gate and the ship. The motor torpedo boat should then enter the lock and fire her torpedoes at the inner gate – torpedoes from which the engines had been removed and replaced by high explosive and which would travel from 100–200 yards under their own momentum after being fired, before striking the bottom where they would explode close to the inner gate, which would then collapse as the tide fell. The Commando, supported by Royal Engineers' Demolition Parties, would then carry out demolition at selected points in the dockyard, before falling back on the lock. Meanwhile the four motor launches would have entered the lock and secured alongside under the shelter of its walls. The men would immediately embark in the motor launches, in which they would return to England, being covered when clear of the coast by two or three Hunt-class destroyers.

We explained our ideas a few days later to Mountbatten, who approved them in principle after a short discussion.

Before the end of January, the Admiralty had provisionally chosen H.M.S. *Campbeltown* – an old ex-American destroyer – to be the expendable ship, and her Captain (at that time Lord Teynham) came to see me for a short discussion on 28 January.

During February we finalised the outline plan fixing the date for the raid for 28 March, which Mountbatten then laid before the Chiefs of Staff, who approved it without delay. Force Commanders were at once appointed – Commander R.E.D. Ryder (later Captain Ryder, V.C.) for the Navy, and Lieutenant Colonel Newman, who was in command of the Commando selected for the operation, and who was later awarded the V.C. for his part in the raid.

On 26 February we had a long meeting with the Assistant Chief of Naval Staff for Home Operations (Rear Admiral Power), and Admiral of the Fleet Sir Charles Forbes, Commander-in-Chief, Plymouth, within whose command the craft for the operation would assemble and be trained. Admiral Forbes had been shown the outline plan immediately after a meeting on another subject that he had attended during the forenoon. When we re-assembled to discuss St. Nazaire, the Admiral immediately opened the discussion with these words: 'Well, I congratulate you, Gentlemen; so long as you don't mind having every ship in the raiding force sunk and every soldier killed, I am sure it will be a great success.'

Admiral Mountbatten immediately countered this gloomy forecast by saying to the Admiral: 'Oh, by the way, I must introduce you, Admiral, to Colonel Newman, who will be in command of the troops, and Commander Ryder who will be in command of the ships.' The Admiral blushed and said no more.

It was during this meeting that a telephone call to the Admiral at the R.N. College at Dartmouth took place, saying that fighter bombers had just attacked. Admiral Forbes decided there and then that the Cadets must be moved to a safer place. Mountbatten immediately asked whether he could have Dartmouth for Combined Operations landing craft training. This was agreed, and a most valuable base it formed to be.

According to the method which Mountbatten had originally envisaged for the planning, mounting and execution of raids, my own involvement in the St. Nazaire raid ought to have ceased at this point. Mountbatten's idea had been that the three "Advisers" and their Operational Staffs should produce outline plans under my chairmanship, these to be submitted to him and he would seek approval to go ahead from the Chiefs of Staff Committee. As soon as this was obtained, Force Commanders would be appointed and the outline plan handed to them with instructions to produce detailed operational orders within the framework of the approved outline. For this purpose, they would be given office accommodation in C.O.H.Q. and could call upon the Technical and Training Staff of the Combined Operations Command for the craft and troops required, and for training facilities.

Meanwhile, the planners at C.O.H.Q. would be free to go ahead with plans for another raid. This, on a small scale, was the principle on which the "Great German General Staff" had always functioned, and it was criticised by many senior officers, including the First Sea Lord, on the grounds that officers who plan an operation should always do so in the knowledge that they would have to carry it out. There is some weight in this criticism because there is an undoubted risk that officers who only plan from the remoteness of Whitehall will get more and more out of touch with the realities of warfare. Against this it is equally true that Mountbatten's method was the only one which could and did enable a succession of highly specialised operations, like the cross-Channel raids, to be planned and carried out in a short space of time.

However, in the case of the St. Nazaire and Bayonne raids, things did not turn out at all as had been intended. To begin with, Sir Charles Forbes (who had no responsibility for any part of the raid except for providing training facilities), strongly opposed the idea of blowing up the *Campbeltown* while the troops and ship's company were taking shelter near the lock side. He said that his "Passive Defence Officer" had advised him that everyone within half a mile would be killed by the blast.

I pointed out in vain that they would be shielded by the earth and masonry between them and the charge, which would be at least 10' below ground level, and furthermore, that we had already consulted the two top experts on blast at the Ministry of Home Security, who had advised that our plan was perfectly safe. The Admiral replied that they must be civilians, and insisted that the charge should not be exploded until an hour after the troops had been withdrawn. This meant that the motor torpedo boat with special torpedoes could not enter the lock to destroy the inner gate, thus making the whole great basin tidal.

Worse was to follow. Colonel Newman objected to having "all his eggs in one basket" and pressed that the Commando should be embarked in motor launches and landed at a number of different points in the dockyard, and Ryder at one time went so far as to question the need for an expendable ship at all. It was in vain that we pointed out that motor launches were made of wood and driven by petrol and the chances of achieving surprise with an armada of eighteen coastal craft were slim, and hence they would all most probably be blazing wrecks before they got alongside at all. Yet such was the deference paid to Newman and Ryder simply because they were going to do the job that they nearly got their way, and would have done so had not Mountbatten made it clear that C.O.H.Q. would have nothing more to do with the operation unless the expendable ship remained its central feature.

A compromise was eventually reached, whereby part of the Commando went in the *Campbeltown,* and part was split up between a number of motor launches. In the event our worst fears were confirmed and few of the troops got ashore from the motor launches, while the number of craft in company with *Campbeltown* betrayed her intention to the German gunners sooner than would have occurred had she been accompanied by only four motor launches and one M.T.B. which could have remained concealed from the shore by keeping a station close on her starboard side. In consequence, *Campbeltown* came under heavier fire than we had expected and the troops on board suffered heavier casualties before they landed than we had hoped for.

The decision to delay exploding the great charge of high explosive naturally saved the inner gate from destruction, although all its pumping machinery was effectively put out of action by the demolition parties. It brought, however, one unforeseen dividend. For reasons never explained the charge failed to detonate until the following afternoon, by which time a large party of German V.I.P.s. had assembled on board the ship to survey the scene. All perished.

One other point deserves mentioning. In the original plan we had suggested that consideration should be given to synchronising a heavy air raid on St. Nazaire with the final approach of the raiding force, with the object of making the coast defence gunners take cover, and keeping the eyes of the German look-outs on the sky. The idea was an old and very debateable one, because it could equally be argued that an air-raid – especially if ineffective – may have the opposite effect of alerting the guns' crews and lookouts.

But on one point we were definite. There was a Cabinet ruling against blind bombing of French towns. Whenever there was cloud cover the bombers had orders to remain over the target for as long as they could, and failing a visual siting, to return to England and jettison their bombs before landing. Only the Prime Minister himself could relax this rule, and Mountbatten strongly emphasised that unless the Prime Minister was prepared to do so, the air raid should be out of the plan. But Mr. Churchill agreed that in the special circumstances the rule could be relaxed, and as both Newman and Ryder were in favour of a diversionary raid, it was included in the plan.

Through a tragic misunderstanding the Prime Minister's instruction never reached the bombers and when they arrived over St. Nazaire, the whole area was hidden by a great thunderstorm, while remaining almost as light as day in the full moon above the thunderclouds. With great gallantry the bombers remained for sixty-five minutes in the area, frequently diving into the clouds to escape German fighters, and in the hope of seeing the ground. But no bombs were dropped, and the only result of the air raid was the loss of a number of bombers and the alerting of the German garrison and gunners. Nevertheless, the raid achieved its immediate objective of rendering the great lock useless for the rest of the war. More importantly, it caused the Germans to strengthen their defences along the whole Atlantic coast. Indeed, the Admiralty firmly believed, that the destruction of the lock was the reason why the *Tirpitz* never ventured forth into the Atlantic.

Chapter 3

BRUNEVAL AND THE SMALL SCALE RAIDING FORCE

The twin raid on Bayonne was timed for tidal reasons to take place on 4 April. Two complete Commandos plus specialist demolition troops were to take part and were to be embarked in the *Queen Wilhelmina* and the *Princess Beatrix*, two very fine Dutch cross-Channel ships of about 7,000 tons and diesel driven. They were to be escorted by four Hunt-class destroyers.

The crucial problem was how to reach Bayonne undetected, and the plan was to route the force far to the west, roughly along one of the customary Gibraltar convoy routes. On reaching the latitude of Cape Finisterre, the force would turn east and separate, the ships keeping just within visual contact of one another. On reaching the Spanish coast, they would disguise themselves (with the aid of prepared painted canvas back-cloths) as the Spanish cruiser *Canarias* and as a Spanish passenger ship which often cruised in those waters. They were ordered to remain close enough inshore to give any German aircraft the impression that they must be Spanish, but too far off for their disguise to be penetrated by watchers from the shore (that is to say from 10–15 miles offshore).

They duly arrived, undetected, and stopped 12 miles off Bayonne about midnight so as to lower their armoured landing craft outside normal radar detection range. One Commando was to be landed immediately to the north of the river bar, with orders to over-run a large battery of 11″ guns which was sited only some 100 yards from the high-water mark, and apparently protected only by a low grass bank. Most of the remaining landing craft were to cross the river bar and land their troops mainly on the south bank.

Although we knew of some 4,000 German troops being accommodated in the French barracks at Bayonne, they were all new entrants under training, and the Commandos were expected to make short work of them. Furthermore, we relied upon complete surprise, which, indeed, was achieved. The craft making for the battery got so close to the shore that two German sentries could be seen sitting on the grass bank talking to each other and smoking. It was at this moment that the Officer-in-Charge of the landing craft decided that the swell was too great to make beaching the craft, or crossing the river bar advisable, so at the very last moment he made the emergency signal which ordered all craft to turn back and return to their parent ships. This they did with the loss of one craft, which was damaged whilst being hoisted, and then sunk to avoid delay.

Throughout all this time there was no reaction from the enemy. One of the objectives of the raid had been to destroy as many as possible of the specialised ore carriers which carried the valuable black iron ore (Fe304) from northern Spain to Bayonne, the terminal port in France. These vessels could only enter Bayonne in fair weather, and it was known that when held up by gales they assembled and waited in the Bay at St. Jean de Luz.

Accordingly, the Naval Commander had orders to visit this bay and sink any ore ships which might be at anchor in it. However, the weather having been fair, the bay was empty. Nevertheless, two destroyers were sent in to bombard St. Jean de Luz. Even this did not betray the purpose of the raiding force, because German reconnaissance aircraft mistook the *Queen Wilhelmina* and the *Princess Beatrix* for special anti-aircraft ships sent to escort the destroyers. So, the force returned to England without incident, having achieved nothing whatsoever.

During the weeks when we were busy with preparations for the raids on St. Nazaire and Bayonne, the raid on Bruneval was carried out with complete success, but the one planned on the Ostend front had to be cancelled because it proved impossible to clear the minefields in that area.

Despite its small scale, the raid on Bruneval was a remarkable achievement which created a profound impression throughout Europe and especially in France. It was the first time in the history of warfare that troops had been parachuted onto a strongly fortified objective, and then withdrawn by sea. It moreover achieved its objective by enabling radio countermeasures to be taken against the latest German anti-aircraft system from the outset. Meanwhile, the outline plan for seizing Alderney, and also for the June raid on Dieppe, were approved by the Chiefs of Staff Committee, and active preparations on both began. In view, however, of the scale of the Dieppe raid, the Prime Minister entered a caveat that the Army part of the plan should be scrutinised by a General nominated by the Commander-in-Chief, Home Force. General Paget nominated General Montgomery with the results that will be described later.

This work alone kept C.O.H.Q. extremely busy, but more important was the long-term logistic planning which had to be carried out concurrently. As far back as 26 February a meeting attended by the Naval Commanders-in-Chief, plus senior representatives from the Admiralty and the Ministry of Shipping, was held at C.O.H.Q. to discuss the re-opening and re-equipment of the South Coast Ports in preparation for a major invasion across the Channel. The code-name *Round-up* had already been allocated to the invasion of France and an outline plan had been prepared by the Future Operational Planning Section (F.O.P.S. – sometimes irreverently called 'The Futile Operational Planning Section') for the operation which was visualised as taking place in 1943, but the more we looked at the F.O.P.S. plan the less we liked it, because it assumed that only the troops needed for the spearhead of the assault need be carried in specialised landing ships and craft. The ensuing build-up of forces and stores were to go in large merchant vessels. Somehow, we could not picture a great number of passenger and cargo liners lying solemnly at anchor off the enemy coast, while troops, guns and vehicles were laboriously hoisted out and ferried ashore.

In this connection I had accompanied Mountbatten in February, while he inspected Commandos in the Inverary area, and afterwards to watch a rehearsal for the planned landings to be made in Madagascar. We had both been horrified at the dilatory conduct of the "Docks Operating Companies" who carried out the embarkation and disembarkation of all the troops' equipment from heavy tanks or S.P. Artillery, i.e., mobile guns or S.P.A., down to the dentist's caravan. The troops who carried out the rehearsal (who, as things turned out were not those who carried out the operation!) were part of the formation called the "Expeditionary Force" under the command of Lieutenant General Alexander (Now Field Marshal Earl Alexander). I was particularly shocked at the slow-motion act put on by the Docks Operating Companies, who were in fact dockers dressed up as soldiers.

Alex told us that nothing was likely to hasten them. He had bitter memories of Gallipoli where, as a young officer he had watched our soldiers dying through lack of supplies and ammunition, while the men unloading stores from the supply ships offshore knocked off regularly for their tea breaks and meal hours, and took cover so long as a single Turkish aircraft was in sight. The General said we should never do any good with them and advised that any plan to invade France had best exclude them.

I think it fair to say that it was on our way back to London the two days later that Mountbatten and I agreed to aim for sufficient "White Ensign" landing craft to lift a big enough Army to secure a firm lodgement in France from which a major offensive could be launched in due course. Previously the use of commissioned landing craft had only been visualised for the assault and immediate follow-up phase of the operation. The implications of this decision were most serious, because they involved the construction of landing craft and landing ships on a scale hitherto undreamt of.

I mentioned that the troops who rehearsed the landings at Madagascar were not those who carried out the operation. A strange story lies behind this curious fact. Originally Mountbatten had proposed the employment of the Royal Marine Division, together with No.5 Commando, for this operation. The Royal Marine Divisional Commander, Major General Bob Sturges was therefore nominated as the Force Commander, and this was put to the Prime Minister and was approved by him, but no decision was taken at the time about the composition of the forces, although the rehearsal was carried out by the Royal Marine Division, while the 29th and 72nd Infantry Brigades provided the opposition.

After the rehearsal the operation was stood down for security reasons. It was suddenly re-mounted a few weeks later, but the C.I.G.S. (General Alanbrooke) having discovered that the Royal Marine Division had no "tail" and were unable to provide one themselves, refused to accept them for the operation. But he had to accept the Royal Marine Commander, because this had already been approved by the Prime Minister. And so, we had the odd situation of the Royal Marine Divisional Commander and his Headquarters Staff commanding an Army operation which was carried out by the 29th and 72nd Brigades, who had furnished the opposition at the rehearsal.

Needless to say, Mountbatten protested strongly about this treatment of the Royal Marines, but the C.I.G.S. was adamant: they must make up their minds, he argued, that they would never be given a tail by the Army and would thus stand no chance of ever being employed as a division in an operational role. This caused consternation among the Royal Marines, who then offered their division to General Eisenhower. Some weeks later, however, Eisenhower turned the division over to the Combined Operations Command, and it was then affiliated to "Force J". The lack of tail mattered less so long as the division was employed mainly on Combined Operations training, with the prospect of an occasional raid.

Even so, neither the Royal Marines, nor the Guards Armoured Division were able, officially "to move themselves". The Army, backed by Major General Holmes, its Director of Movements, had made very heavy weather of this, and even units as small as a Brigade were not supposed to move from A to B without the guidance of a small army of "Movement Officers". Fortunately, I had my own Naval Staff, some officers who were fully capable of moving anything up to a division, and nobody seemed to mind.

However this may be, Mountbatten felt strongly, and I think rightly, that the long term future of the Royal Marines lay in breaking up their divisions into Commandos, and this was done. At the time the policy was strongly opposed by nearly all the conventionally minded senior officers in the Royal Marines. Yet the policy has stood the test of time. Royal Marine Commandos have fought with distinction in many parts of the world, and had it not been for their existence the whole Corps might well have been disbanded by now.

By March 1942 the Government were under heavy pressure both from Russia and the United States of America to open a second front in the West (by which they meant France) during the summer of 1942. All responsible people in England were opposed to any such undertaking. But on 6 March, Mountbatten received an urgent Minute from the Prime Minister asking for his opinion on what could be done if it became imperative to carry out a holding operation in France in, say, July 1942, with the object of keeping Russia in the war. He added that a similar Minute had been addressed to the Commander-in-Chief, Home Forces, and to the Chiefs of Staff Committee.

Mountbatten instructed me to draft a reply for discussion the following day. My mind went back to Monty's solution to General Alanbrooke's Staff Exercise the previous December and January. I therefore drafted quite a short paper, whose main conclusions were:

(i) That a holding operation was possible providing it took the form of attacking and holding the Cherbourg Peninsula.

(ii) If all went exceedingly well, we might consider an attack to re-capture the Channel Islands once the Cherbourg Peninsula was secure.

This reply was discussed very fully during the forenoon of 7 March, with Mountbatten in the Chair, and was agreed subject to minor amendments. It was sent to the Prime Minister at about noon.

Meanwhile, we warned that both General Paget and the Chiefs of Staff had turned the whole idea down flat. Late on the same day the C.I.G.S. came to C.O.H.Q. and had a long private discussion with Mountbatten.

On the following day, 8 March, Mountbatten informed us that he was to become "Chief of Combined Operations" instead of "Adviser" with the acting rank of Vice Admiral, and the honorary rank of Lieutenant General and Air Marshal. More important, he was to attend all Chiefs of Staff Meetings at which combined operations were likely to be discussed, which meant in practice all of them. Furthermore he, Mountbatten, had also been instructed to nominate a Major General as Vice Chief of Combined Operations, an Air Marshal as Deputy Chief, and a senior Captain as Assistant Chief, with the rank of Commodore Second Class. He was kind enough to ask me to accept the latter appointment. However, rightly or wrongly, I asked to be excused. The Navy has always hated "acting" ranks, and I was, after all, a very junior Captain, and I felt sure I should carry no more weight as a Commodore on his staff than as a Captain. Eventually the appointment went to Captain R.M. Ellis, a brilliant officer who had distinguished himself as the Captain of H.M.S. *Suffolk* during the chase of the *Bismarck*.

Under the new organisation, Ellis was to be concerned mostly with logistic planning for major operations, while I continued to be responsible for the planning of raids. But we never had rigid demarcation over major operations. In contrast very few officers at C.O.H.Q. were in on the raids for obvious reasons of security. Air Marshal James Robb was appointed as Deputy Chief, and his work was similar to that of Captain Willetts, though he naturally carried more weight because of his rank and personality.

This startling upgrading of C.O.H.Q. in general, and Mountbatten in particular, aroused jealousy and opposition from the Service Departments, and delayed the formal announcement of the appointments until later in the month. From my own point of view, which I think was shared by all who worked at C.O.H.Q., it greatly increased and widened the scope of our work. In particular it enabled us to set forth suggestions for the better conduct of the war in the knowledge that, if agreed by our small operational staff at C.O.H.Q., and by Mountbatten himself, they would be brought to the notice of the Prime Minister and the Chiefs of Staff without delay. The effect on Mountbatten himself was to redouble his energy and zest for work.

The raiding programme was not affected, but as the projected raids grew in size, so also did the controversy that arose between the three services once Force Commanders had been appointed. Indeed, the abortive raid on Bayonne was destined to be the beginning of weeks of frustration.

The First Guards Brigade, plus a battalion of parachute troops, were selected for the capture of Alderney. Fighter Command was to bear the lion's share of the R.A.F.'s contribution, although the landing was to be immediately preceded by a very heavy night bomber attack. The island made a readily identifiable target and was so small that a saturation bombing was easily within our capabilities. Indeed, Professor Zukerman expressed the opinion that we had asked for too many bombers in our original outline plan. The airborne troops were to be dropped as soon as possible after the bombing was over, and the same applied to the landing of the troops from the sea. In practice I felt that the most difficult part of the operation would be to lead the small and slow "L.C.A." through the very strong cross tides which guard the approaches to the small beaches of the Channel Islands, flanked as they are by shoal water and partly submerged rocks.

According to British practice Joint Commanders were appointed: Air Marshal Leigh-Mallory (then A.O.C. No.11 Group) for the Air, the Commanding Officer of the Guards Brigade for the Army, and Commodore A.W. Clarke for the Navy. In addition, General Browning – the Commander of the Airborne Division – claimed a decisive vote in the detailed planning. Mountbatten had arranged for the Isle of Wight to be sealed – for security purposes, and for the troops plus the combined Signal Unit to be sent there for training. Difficulties arose from the outset over the detailed planning, and it was clear that the Military Commander was reluctant to "chance his arm", or to subject his troops to the great hazards which are inevitable in raiding operations.

The idea of holding Alderney was abandoned by 28 April, and the operation shrank to a medium-sized, and not particularly attractive raid. The point of contention lay in the precise timing. Bomber Command refused to operate after the time at which there was least possibility of bombers being overtaken by daylight, and General Browning refused to allow his troops to be dropped before he was certain there would be enough daylight.

Meanwhile, throughout the whole of April, the planning for the great raid on Dieppe went forward quickly and harmoniously, because the Canadian General Roberts and his staff were eager to chance their arm, and seemed anxious to take on any operation, whatever the risks. Accordingly, it was decided by the end of April to abandon the Alderney operation, if only because we needed to get the Guards Brigade out of the Isle of Wight to make room for the 2nd Canadian Division to go in.

Going back a little in time, on 17 March we had a visitor at C.O.H.Q. in the person of Captain March-Phillipps, a young Army Officer of great gallantry, and with an appalling stammer. Exactly how he gained access to Mountbatten at a time when we were overwhelmed with work, I never knew, but he came with an idea which everyone except Mountbatten and myself at once dismissed as ridiculous. Briefly, his idea was that he should be placed in command of a very small, but self-contained, independent, and permanent raiding force, made up of two Fairmile motor launches and about forty specially selected soldiers. He was to be in sole command; the Naval C.O.s of the craft were to do precisely what he told them, and he was to have authority to carry out very small-scale raids (by perhaps twenty men at the most), chiefly on the Normandy and Brittany coasts, and based on detailed intelligence which would be supplied to him from time to time by C.O.H.Q.

I told Mountbatten that in my opinion the idea was worth pursuing for several reasons. It offered a means of getting away from the system of joint Commanders so beloved of the English and so disliked by the Americans. (March-Phillips was, by the way, a very experienced yachtsman with expert knowledge of the French coast from Cherbourg to Ushant). By keeping the raids small and confining the objectives to points within a mile of most of the landing beaches, it would be possible for each little operation to begin and end during the hours of darkness, thereby obviating the need for fighter cover. One of the major difficulties in planning cross-Channel raids was that even if only one Commando was to be landed, it could, and did, lead to a major air operation to which the whole of Fighter Command had to be committed.

Nevertheless, nobody except myself seemed very keen on March-Phillips's proposal, and even Mountbatten was a little doubtful and asked me to write a paper for submission to the Chiefs of Staff if I really thought the establishment of S.S.R.F. (Small Scale Raiding Force) was worthwhile. Before doing so I had a long talk with March-Phillips and asked him why he wanted motor launches with a full speed of 15 or 16 knots as opposed to 30 knot gunboats, and secondly, how he proposed to get the raiders ashore. His answer to the second question was to carry Goatley boats on deck and let the raiders row or paddle themselves to the beach. He had opted for motor launches partly because he was more likely to get them, and partly because he believed they were far more silent when proceeding dead slow.

These were good answers, and to my mind the great attraction of his general idea was the simplicity and secrecy with which small scale raids could be carried out. But I impressed upon him that his command of the motor launches could only be operational and on no account could he interfere with the discipline or the maintenance of the craft: Furthermore, I was sure that the Naval Commanders-in-Chief would never allow him to operate unless he could prepare operation orders which their Staff Officers could understand, because they must know his whereabouts and intentions every time he put to sea. With reluctance he agreed to these conditions.

I then drafted a paper seeking approval to set the scheme in motion, which Mountbatten submitted to the Chiefs of Staff Committee, who accepted it at once despite some misgivings from the Admiralty. Meanwhile a section of the C.O.H.Q. Staff under Major Antony Head (now the Rt. Hon. Lord Head) was given the task of preparing the intelligence for batches of about twelve possible small-scale raids from which March-Phillips could select and carry out as many as he could. Weeks passed and we heard no more from S.S.R.F. until an infuriated Naval Commander-in-Chief reported that March-Phillips had ordered an unauthorised "Alteration and Addition" to be carried out on the main engine exhausts of the two motor launches, in consequence of which both craft were unserviceable.

To carry out unofficial alterations and additions to His Majesty's Ships is a sin against the light in any circumstances: for a young Army officer to do so with the aid of technical soldiers is to sin against the Holy Ghost. Senior naval officers said this was just the sort of thing to expect from C.O.H.Q. Fortunately for us, and for the future of the S.S.R.F., we had drawn up the directive to March-Phillips with some care and precision, and his action had certainly disregarded it. Besides, it was a foolish one. He had found by experience what we had already warned him, namely that motor launches are not quite so silent as he had thought owing to the exhaust pipes being intermittently under the water. After the breeze had died down and after we had discovered that he was now thinking in terms of raiding parties of only four to eight men, we persuaded him that a high-speed motor torpedo boat would suit his purposes better, and he agreed.

There was available a very fast, but non-operational M.T.B. which for some reason had had its tubes and torpedoes removed, and this craft together with its Commanding Officer, Sub-Lieutenant Bourne, R.N.V.R. was turned over to the Small Scale Raiding Force. Even then, nothing happened until 17 August – two days before the Dieppe raid. By this date I was living pro-tem in the Commander-in-Chief's Portsmouth headquarters on Fort Southwick, and he asked me if I saw any objections to a small-scale raid by six men on the tip of the Cherbourg Peninsula.

I could see no harm from a security point of view, and Admiral James then asked me to take March-Phillips under my orders to get my own staff to write operation orders which the C-in-C's staff could understand, and then use my own discretion on whether to unleash the S.S.R.F. or not. David Luce – by this time my Chief of Staff – was not best pleased at this additional worry just as we were about to set forth on the biggest raid in history, about which March-Phillips, of course, knew nothing.

However, we went ahead, and a little raid was completely successful. All the same, March-Phillips made it clear that the last thing he wanted was to be placed permanently under my operational control. Nevertheless, this is just what happened before the year was out, and before any other small-scale raid took place.

To revert now to the great strategic question that faced us in March, April and May 1942: ought we, or ought we not, to give way to the clamour to open a second front in 1942?

Alone amongst British Military Authorities, the Chief of Combined Operations said it was possible, although highly undesirable unless the landings were in the central Channel area – preferably on the Normandy beaches. Air Chief Marshal Sir Sholto Douglas, Commander-in-Chief, Fighter Command, said that these beaches were too far away, and only the Pas-de-Calais was feasible.

Before this clash of ideas was resolved, the Prime Minister had directed Force Commanders to be appointed: Admiral Ramsay, General Schreiber and Sholto Douglas were selected and a large Joint-Service Staff was established in one of London's bomb-proof underground offices to plan the operation in detail. The code-name *Sledgehammer* was allocated to it. But although C.O.H.Q. had been the originator, in a sense, of the whole idea, and although Mountbatten himself attended some of the *Sledgehammer* meetings when invited, C.O.H.Q. as a whole was not involved. We did, however, undertake some vital logistic preparations which needed to be made before any major cross-Channel operation could be carried out, irrespective of its nature.

The first of these was to re-activate some of the south and south-easterly commercial ports (the Falmouth, Plymouth, Southampton group, and some of the London Docks). The cranes at these ports had been dismantled when France fell and re-erected at Liverpool, Glasgow and other north-west ports. Most of the dock labour had been transferred as well. A plan to get things moving on the south coast had been agreed in outline at the meeting held at C.O.H.Q. on 26 February to which I have already referred. The War Cabinet approved this plan on 20 March.

In addition, it was necessary to construct a large number of concrete ramps on hards at which Landing Craft Tank could be loaded and unloaded in sheltered waters. We also needed an enormously greater lift for food, ammunition and all other stores required to sustain an army once it has established itself ashore and is fighting a campaign. Tank Landing Craft are not essential for this purpose and, of course, we only had enough for the initial assault and immediate "follow-up" on the next tide.

We therefore proposed to requisition some 900 Thames barges, fit them with several outboard engines and a bow door which could be lowered and used as a ramp. These barges could then ply between store ships anchored offshore and beaches, laden with stores and vehicles. The idea was to beach them at high water, wait until the tide fell and they were high and dry, and then let the vehicles drive ashore while the stores would be loaded into other vehicles which would drive out to them across the beach. Since a typical London barge will carry between 50 and 70 tons of cargo, and since there are two tides daily, the total potential lift of 900 barges was enormous.

It would be wrong to pretend that these preparations went smoothly forward. Quite apart from their unconventional nature, every authority under the sun – civil and military alike – claimed the right to have a finger in the pie and refused to co-operate unless they were told exactly what it was all about. Officially, all these problems were the responsibility of the "Director of Transportation" at the War Office: a Major General who so far as I could make out came to some extent under the "Director of Movements" on the General Staff. But responsibility seemed to be vaguely drawn and overlapping. Moreover, the Admiralty and local senior naval officers were actively concerned with the exact positioning of the L.C.T. loading ramps, as also were the local road authorities, and the civil port authorities.

I felt strongly that what was wanted was a "Dictator of Transportation" who, while serving at C.O.H.Q., would have Executive authority to order – not merely request or invite – and who could, when necessary, work at Ministerial level.

Mountbatten agreed with me, but no-one else did – not at first. The problem was to find the man, and somebody suggested Jack Maclay. So, we asked him to visit C.O.H.Q. and discuss the matter. However, although he agreed with the idea, he was expecting shortly to become a Minister of Shipping, and meanwhile did not want to become involved in what was bound to be a highly controversial job. (In the event he got neither job.) After deep thought Mountbatten decided to try to persuade Sir Harold Wernher to take on the job if it was

28

approved. Sir Harold had a well-justified reputation for being a pretty tough businessman.

Among other achievements he had built up a great Electrolux firm. Having secured his co-operation and support the next task was to sell the idea to Sir Edward Bridges, who at once saw its advantages, and then to the Prime Minister. Mountbatten took me to a meeting on the subject, at which Winston fixed me with his eye and asked 'Are you the young man who wants a Dictator of Transportation? Don't you know we are fighting this war to end Dictatorships? We will call him a "Co-ordinator". It comes to much the same thing and sounds better.' When Mountbatten went on to propose Sir Harold Wernher, Winston said, 'Is he not your brother-in-law? I object to nepotism.' To which Mountbatten replied, 'No, he is my brother's brother-in-law, and not my son-in-law.' Winston, who had just appointed Duncan Sandys to an important post, went rather red and there was an ominous silence, but Sir Harold's appointment went forward. And so, Sir Harold Wernher moved to C.O.H.Q. and worked wonders. (His official title was Co-ordinator of Ministerial and Service Facilities (C.M.S.F.)).

The landing hards were completed by the end of June and the barges, after being fitted out, were manned by London bargees who were called up as Naval Ratings for the duration. But despite the uniform, they still looked and talked like bargees. However, they proved highly efficient. The whole organisation came under a senior retired naval captain (Captain Harrison-Wallis), who was one of the rare examples of a senior naval officer who had retired and gone into business and made a great success of it. The main base for the barges was established on the Isle of Wight in temporary buildings commissioned as H.M.S. *Manadon*.

I remember in 1945 when I was the Commodore commanding "Force J" with headquarters at Cowes, and the Senior Naval Officer on the island, being told that a young Ordinary Seaman from H.M.S. *Manadon* had asked to see me to appeal against a sentence of three months' detention passed on him by his Commanding Officer. Such appeals are extremely rare and are usually dealt with on paper. However, as this young man had specially asked to see me, and as his Commanding Officer also wanted me to see him, I did so. It transpired that a Petty Officer had been knocked cold by the young offender after "a bit of an argument". He pleaded extreme provocation, but refused to tell me what the petty officer had called him: he simply could not repeat the words because they had shocked him so.

The bargee Petty Officer had no such inhibitions, and added tolerantly: 'You can see the lad was not brought up on the river, but,

Christ, Sir, someone has taught him how to punch.' 'But I bear him no malice, Sir,' he went on, and then shook hands with the prisoner. Feeling that the case was not going quite as visualised in the Naval Discipline Act, I intervened to explain that mere words could never be sufficient provocation to justify assault, and that young ratings who lose their temper should in any case refrain from singling out a Petty Officer to attack. 'But, Sir,' pleaded the Ordinary Seaman, 'I can hardly help that. You see I'm the only man on *Manadon* who is not a Petty Officer.' This was a slight exaggeration, but only a slight one. It transpired that all the bargees had been entered as Petty Officers. Fortunately, I was able to find a legal flaw in the proceedings leading up to this particular conviction, and therefore set it aside.

All these preparations cannot have passed unobserved by the enemy, so we felt that they might at least serve as a deception plan and cause some reinforcements to the German troops in France and thus ease the pressure on the Russians. And yet, in actual fact, the *Sledgehammer* plan never looked like getting off the ground, and I am sure it was a profound mistake to have appointed Force Commanders before a firm decision had been reached on whether to attack in the central Channel or the Pas-de-Calais. But the mistake was about to be repeated on a bigger and more time-consuming scale.

Whether or not the Germans were being deceived by our massive logistical preparations we could not tell at the time, but we certainly could not deceive our American allies, or for that matter the Russians. Accordingly, under pressure from the Prime Minister, a body was set up called "The Combined Commanders" which comprised the Commander-in-Chief, Home Forces himself, Air Chief Marshal Sholto Douglas C.-in-C. Fighter Command, and the Chief of Combined Operations. The Combined Commanders were instructed to draw up a plan for full scale invasion in 1943, or, in other words, to revise and bring up-to-date a plan for Operation *Round-up*.

This brought the C.O.H.Q. staff fully into the picture and took up a great deal of our time. For myself, I could not take the work very seriously. The combined staffs of the Combined Commanders were so large that when they held plenary meetings it resembled a meeting of Parliament itself, with no equivalent to Mr. Speaker to enforce rules of Order. Yet I kept in touch and kept Commodore Ellis in touch, who was more and more taking the lead in logistic preparations. Indeed, it is true to say that almost every novel idea which was later used in Operation *Overlord* (that is to say during the real invasion in 1944) originated in C.O.H.Q during April 1942 – most of them from Commodore Ellis's fertile brain.

Notable exceptions to this generalisation included the artificial harbours, the rocket craft, and the use of Army 25-pounders to swell the bombardment of beach areas by firing them from L.C.T. during the run-in. I contributed one or two ideas myself, because although I dislike anybody interfering with my own work, I felt no inhibitions about interfering with the work of others. It was, for example, on my suggestion that Coasters of up to 2,000 tons were trained to run themselves aground at high water so that their cargoes could be unloaded into lorries when they were high and dry at low water.

The supply of petrol posed a problem, because while the laying of pipelines on the sea bed was an obvious solution from the outset, and ensured the bulk supply, the Army also had to have a large proportion in 4-gallon jerry-cans for operational reasons. We did not think there would be time to organise a transfer on the beachhead during the early stages of the assault. I therefore proposed that these drums should be carried as a deck cargo in small coasters, which should steam parallel to the beach at high water and throw their deck cargo overboard at about the half tide line. Later the 4-gallon cans could be collected by lorries when the tide fell. This method had the merits of simplicity and comparative safety.

In early April a most important event occurred. The "Marshall Conversations", as they came to be called, were opened in London and lasted for five days. By this time, it was evident to all "in the know" that Operation *Sledgehammer* had run into the sands and would never take place save possibly as a "sacrifice operation", against which the Prime Minister had firmly and rightly set his face. Far more serious were the growing doubts about the prospects for *Round-up* in 1943. The Combined Commanders were no nearer to agreement about even an outline plan. At first, they were inclined to treat Mountbatten as if he were a Naval Force Commander – an attitude which he corrected by persuading the Chiefs of Staff to appoint Admiral Ramsay in that capacity.

Yet, although none could have been more familiar with the difficulties that would face slow landing craft in the strong tidal streams of the Strait of Dover, and with the tremendous strength of the German heavy batteries in the Calais/Boulogne area, the Admiral seemed more anxious to avoid conflict with his colleagues than in the production of a serious and practicable plan. Eventually the Chiefs of Staff Committee at Mountbatten's instigation requested the Combined Commanders to produce an outline plan by the first week in April. Their plan was drafted without consultation with Mountbatten and involved an assault in the Pas-de-Calais area.

At the meeting of the Chiefs of Staff Committee to discuss this plan, Mountbatten attended in a dual capacity, and again left no-one in any doubt about his strong and consistent opposition to landing to the east of the Normandy beaches. After a long discussion his view prevailed, and the Combined Commanders were instructed to draw up a new plan based on landings in the central Channel. Very senior officers, like General Paget and Air Chief Marshal Sholto Douglas, were understandably angry and humiliated although they had only themselves to blame.

At the next meeting of the Combined Commanders with their big staffs and consequently in the presence of a mass of junior Staff Officers, the Commander-in-Chief, Home Forces opened the proceedings with a bitter attack on the Chief of Combined Operations, implying that his conduct had been disloyal and insubordinate. Fortunately, Mountbatten was young enough to keep his temper, and quietly deployed once again the reasons why C.O.H.Q. would have nothing to do with a plan to assault in the Pas-de-Calais area. He added that he and his staff had always pointed out that the Pas-de-Calais would never do, and that he had only said to the Chiefs of Staff what he had said over and over again to the Combined Commanders.

By this time there were American military observers involved, and it must have seemed to them that *Round-up*, like *Sledgehammer*, was going to be a non-starter; an opinion strengthened by the Prime Minister's known pre-occupation with the position in Africa; his concern for the safety of India, and his long flirtation for striking through Italy at what he erroneously believed would be 'the soft under-belly of Europe'.

General Marshall, the President's principal military adviser, and a warm advocate of a policy of winning the European War first and striking at Japan second, had therefore been sent to England at the head of a powerful U.S. mission to set forth the American views on what strategy should be followed in 1942 and 1943. His object was to pin us down to *Round-up*, and if possible, to keep *Sledgehammer* alive as well.

The Chairman of the Conference, nominated by the Prime Minister, was Oliver Stanley, a Privy Councillor and ex-Minister, who held an appointment with the delightful title of "The Controller of Deception" – and a wonderful Chairman he made.

General Marshall was asked to make an opening statement. After explaining his support for tackling Hitler first, despite the weight of American public opinion which favoured going first for Japan, he went on to develop the case for opening a second front in north-west France, and he ended with words which I shall never forget: 'It is therefore,

Gentlemen, the considered opinion of the United States Administration that unless H.M. Government are in broad agreement, the war in Europe cannot usefully be pursued.' In the hush that followed anyone on our side of the Atlantic who may have fancied a little strategical kite-flying, desisted!

There followed working meetings to discuss the plan at which Colonel Wedemeyer took the Chair for the Americans and Mountbatten for the British.

The Americans explained that they visualised about forty-eight divisions being committed to the operation which would take place in 1943. The build-up in the United Kingdom of those American troops that were required in the early stages of the operation must therefore begin at once. The code-name *Bolero* was given to it. Naturally we pressed them about landing craft, and they gave us figures for the number of tank landing ships and tank landing craft likely to be available, which accorded more or less with what we ourselves would have considered necessary. But they added that the bulk of the infantry would have to be carried in small landing craft personnel (L.C.P.), of which 7,000 would be available and afloat crossing the Channel on D-Day.

We suggested that so great a reliance on L.C.P. would make the operation unduly dependent on fine weather and, furthermore, that it would be impracticable to control so great a number. We went on to explain that similar considerations had led us to design the "Giant Eureka", although it was primarily intended for raids. However, only thirty, with a total lift of 3,600 troops were being built, and the first of these craft would not be ready until June 1943.

The Americans were tremendously interested in the "Giant Eureka", and some of them adjourned to meet in C.O.H.Q. where Mr Merrington explained the design in some detail. Colonel Wedemeyer then drafted a signal for General Marshall to send to the President, describing the need for "Giant Eurekas" but adding one more requirement: namely the ability to cross the Atlantic in winter. The requirement for this craft was put at a total lift of about 100,000 men. The signal was sent off the same evening.

Two or three days later, at a final session, General Marshall announced that he had received a message from the President agreeing to this particular proposal and adding that an outline design had already been completed, and orders placed. Each craft would carry some 300 men, and two flotillas of twelve craft each would be sent over to the United Kingdom in the April of 1943 – that was to say in only twelve months' time. This timetable was kept, and no single incident could illustrate more dramatically the vast industrial resources of the U.S.A. or the speed with which they could be mobilised, or the measureless power of the President.

During his stay in London, General Marshall attended a meeting of the Chiefs of Staff at which he expressed a wish to visit C.O.H.Q. He came with Colonel Wedemeyer and was taken round the various offices, ending up in Mountbatten's own office. He then said how astonished he had been to see officers of all three Services working together as a single team, often in the same room and on the same project. How had this been achieved? Mountbatten replied that, after all, they all spoke the same language, and were fighting on the same side. He added that, since this went for the Americans as well, why not send over some U.S. soldiers, sailors and airmen to join the C.O.H.Q. staff. The General jumped at the idea, shortly afterwards General Truscott joined us at the head of an American Three-Service Staff. Thus C.O.H.Q. had what was perhaps the first permanent and integrated international staff.

Before leaving, General Marshall made it clear that without prejudice to *Round-up* in 1943, the U.S. Administration were still not reconciled to the British decision to abandon *Sledgehammer* in 1942. Accordingly, the *Sledgehammer* Force Commanders were re-activated a few days afterwards. By a strange turn of fortune, the Combined Staff working on *Sledgehammer* ended up planning the North Africa Landings under General Eisenhower.

These varied activities made April 1942 an exceptionally busy month for C.O.H.Q., but for the second half of the month I myself was increasingly pre-occupied with the planning and preparations for the Dieppe raid. In theory the large staffs who worked for the "Combined Commanders" and at the *Sledgehammer* plan had nothing to do with raids, and Mountbatten was so deeply concerned to preserve secrecy in this field that no officer could attend a Planning Meeting about a raid without a special pass bearing the code-name of the raid in question. But whenever you assemble a big staff to plan for the distant future, gossip is inevitable.

I was therefore disturbed, but not surprised, when a Home Forces Brigadier approached me one day and said he would like to have a word about our proposed raid on Dieppe. He went on to explain that one plan he was examining for *Round-up* involved an initial simultaneous attack on four or five small ports between Boulogne and St. Brieux. The attacks would be tactically independent, one division being committed to each. Subsequently, during the follow-up and build-up, each division would be reinforced and its bridge-head developed, depending on how things went.

He went on to say that each divisional assault was to be based on identical tactics about which there was some division of opinion in the Home Forces Staff. However, the current idea was to deliver flank attacks, each of Brigade strength, while the third Brigade would be held back as a floating reserve ready to reinforce one of the flank attacks, or to deliver a frontal assault timed to synchronise with the approach of one or both of the flank Brigades from the landward side of the seaport. 'Would it be possible,' he asked, 'so to plan the Dieppe raid, which was, after all, intended primarily to gain experience, that these tactics could be tested?' I replied that this was not for me to say, but I would put the matter to Charles Haydon in time for it to be discussed at our next planning meeting.

The General's first reaction, like my own, was anxiety that Dieppe should already – in the first half of April – be a matter of common knowledge to the big Staffs of the Combined Commanders. That was by now beyond our control; on the merits of the proposal, however, Charles Haydon felt that there were attractive features to putting the main weight of our assault on the flanks. The major problems and uncertainties of an invasion could be tested equally well by avoiding an initial frontal attack, and the risk to the troops if the landings were held up would be greatly lessened. And so, the C.O.H.Q. plan went forward on these lines, and was provisionally approved in outline by the Chiefs of Staff subject to the Prime Minister's caveat, which I have already mentioned, that the Army part of the plan must be vetted by a Commanding General nominated by General Paget.

Monty, still Commander-in-Chief, South Eastern Command at that time, was nominated. He lost no time in asking for a preliminary informal meeting so that he and his staff could clear their minds on one or two points. This meeting (held I think in my room at C.O.H.Q.), was attended by about nine officers.

We had the impression that the General would only send a representative, and that any discussion would, in diplomatic parlance, be of an exploratory nature. It therefore occurred to no-one to suggest that Mountbatten himself should attend, and I myself only went because Charles Haydon felt it would be better, since it was his part of the plan that was under scrutiny, and I should be there to take the Chair. In the event Monty came himself and at once said to me: 'This is a C.O.H.Q. plan, so please take the Chair.' Nevertheless, he needed little persuasion to take it himself. Coming directly to the point, he opened the Meeting by saying that the Military part of the plan was 'the work of an amateur!' If it was a fact (and indeed it was a fact), that we could only allow troops to remain ashore for a maximum of 15 hours, then it would be impossible for the flank brigades to work round and reach Dieppe from the landward side in the time. This would still be true, even if there were no Germans to oppose them. He pointed out that the only way the town and seaport could be captured quickly was to deliver a frontal assault and take it by coup-de-main.

'Would it be possible for the Navy to land the major part of a division simultaneously on the sea front of the town, with two or three battalions on the beach at Pourville, some two or three miles to the south, together with another battalion at Puys, albeit a mile to the north?' I replied and subsequently confirmed that a completely simultaneous landing would hardly be practicable as there would be insufficient sea room with so many landing craft to form up in the dark without great risk of confusion. If, however, it was acceptable to have a 20-minute delay between the landings at the centre and on the flanks, then this would be possible from a Naval point of view. The General said that a 20-minute interval was too small to matter, and he then asked that we should re-plan the raid on these lines in conjunction with one or two members of his own staff.

Shortly after the amended plan was ready, a further meeting, at which Mountbatten himself presided, was held to discuss the new plan and compare it with our original plan. At this meeting (which I was unable myself to attend), Mountbatten made it quite clear that he and his staff strongly preferred the original plan. It was pointed out in vain to him that so far as the main object of the raid was concerned, it really did not matter very much whether Dieppe was captured or not, and that this would make but little difference to the main purpose of the operation, namely, to gain experience. Monty, however, remained adamant, and pointed out (with perfect truth, as events showed) that if we did not capture the town the operation would be represented for ever afterwards as a failure, and that from the intelligence at our disposal, there should not be any great difficulty in a frontal assault.

Shortly afterwards Monty got the agreement of General Paget and the C.I.G.S. for the employment of the 2nd Canadian Division on the raid. This settled the choice of the Military Force Commander; namely Major General J.H. Roberts, who was in command of the division. Air Vice Marshal Leigh-Mallory was appointed, as on previous occasions, as the Air Force Commander, and Rear Admiral H.T. Baillie-Grohman was appointed as the Naval Force Commander. One more key planning meeting was held early in June, at which Monty himself took the chair, and at which the Force Commanders were present.

Neither Mountbatten nor I attended this meeting because we were both in Washington. But it was at this meeting that the decision was taken to omit a preliminary night bombing raid during the night before the landings. This decision was taken at the request of the Air and Military Force Commanders. Their reasons were quite different. General Roberts was afraid that the narrow streets leading inland from the sea front would be blocked by fallen masonry, thus preventing his tanks from making progress. Leigh-Mallory, on the other hand, was afraid that Dieppe was too small a target for night bombing and that most of the bombs would fall in the sea, or inland. In his book of memoirs published in 1958, Monty strongly criticises the decision to have no night bombing, but the fact remains that he was in the chair at the meeting which made that decision.

When Mountbatten returned to England round about 10 June he learned for the first time of this important change in the original plan and expressed his disagreement in the strongest terms. By then, however, it was too late to change it. Accordingly, detailed planning went forward with enthusiasm on the outline plan as amended. In contrast to the abortive raid on Alderney, the soldiers were, if anything, over confident. Indeed, General Roberts was eager for action at all costs, and gave the impression of being prepared to take anything on. His chief fear (shared I am bound to say by myself) was that on one excuse or another this operation would join the list of those that failed to take place.

Indeed, the General's fear on this score was reflected in an unwillingness to press for special equipment, or anything which might be made the excuse for cancelling the operation. For example, I myself was most uneasy at the Army's primitive ideas about the demolition of the sea wall. It was important that gaps should be blown, through which tanks could pass. But the Army's technique for achieving this depended upon the troops manhandling "Bangalore Torpedoes" which would be carried in tank landing craft and lugged ashore up to the sea wall. It seemed to me that the soldiers entrusted with this task would be sitting ducks. We therefore urged that some well armoured, but obsolescent heavy tanks should be filled with explosives and driven up the beach to the sea wall, where the soldiers could jump out and take cover while they were blown up. If only this course had been adopted the outcome might have been very different.

By the end of the first week in June, all the preliminary planning was complete, and the Forces were ready to begin their initial training and rehearsal for the operation whose date had been fixed for 20 June. From this stage onwards the story of Dieppe has been told and re-told. Probably the most accurate and detailed account is to be found in the first of Colonel Stacey's *Histories of the Canadian Army in the Second War,* which was published in 1948. I shall make no attempt to give a detailed account in this book. But I shall come back to the raid in a later chapter to describe what happened, purely from my own personal point of view, and to make a few comments on the lessons that were learned.

Meanwhile I must digress to say a word about Mountbatten's visit to Washington, for most of which I accompanied him. He crossed the Atlantic independently in General Eisenhower's private aircraft, while a Lieutenant Colonel Price of C.O.H.Q. and myself travelled with one or two junior Staff Officers from C.O.H.Q. and took the flying boat route via Southern Ireland. This involved a train travelling to Bristol, followed by a flight to an aerodrome near Dunraven, from which we proceeded by car, and rested at the "Dunraven Arms".

As darkness fell (very late because of double summer time and the westerly longitude) the whole party – which included on this occasion Mr Oliver Littleton, Mr Fairy, and a big team of officials from the Ministry of Aircraft Production – drove to Lough Foyle and embarked in a flying boat. As soon as darkness was falling the flying boat took off and proceeded to Baltimore, being routed via Newfoundland. It was considered unsafe to take off in daylight for fear of German long-range fighters; on the other hand, the flying boats were not equipped for taking off in pitch darkness. Because Ireland was neutral, all Service Officers had to travel in plain clothes and were supplied with civilian passports. Our uniform was packed in our suitcases. By a "Gentleman's Agreement" these were never opened by the Irish Customs officials. They did, however, have little bets between themselves as to whether we were Army, Navy or Air Force.

On the day I travelled, which was 1 June, the weather was quite perfect, and I went with a young civil servant for a long walk in Dunraven Park. When about 3 miles from the village we suddenly realised we were being followed by two young Irishmen dressed in the most exotic uniforms. At first, we feared they might belong to the I.R.A. and as we were both carrying brief cases filled with secret documents, we were somewhat concerned. After a few minutes of anxious doubt, we decided to turn round and confront our shadowers. They fortunately, as they were quick to point out themselves, did not belong to the I.R.A.

On the contrary, they were part of a small private bodyguard organisation, paid by the Manageress of the Dunraven Arms. It appeared that this route to America was regarded in the village as a veritable goldmine, especially when bad weather delayed flights and left the little inn packed with travellers on the way to, or from, Washington. Accordingly, the job of the private bodyguard was to guard against some unfortunate incident of murder or kidnap which might cause the British Government to close the route.

The probable purpose of our small mission to Washington was to convince the United States Administration once and for all that nothing but harm would come of an attempted major operation in 1942, and that in consequence there was no prospect of such an operation being undertaken. I accompanied Mountbatten at two or three long meetings with senior American Staff Officers to explain the logistics and our reasoning. We ended up with a discussion at which the Combined Chiefs of Staff were present in person, and which lasted for between two and three hours. I certainly got the impression, which was shared by Mountbatten, that we had at length convinced them.

Later the same day Mountbatten attended a dinner and discussion with the President himself, which lasted from 20.00 hours until 02.00 hours. The following morning, he told me that he felt quite sure Mr Roosevelt had at last accepted the British point of view. When I returned to England on the following day (leaving Mountbatten behind to watch some Army exercises), I duly reported to this effect to the Prime Minister's Private Secretary and to the First Sea Lord. Unfortunately, it turned out that our impressions were quite wrong, and that the Americans remained wholly unconvinced by our arrangements. The Prime Minister pulled our legs about this saying that it was not unusual for Ambassadors to fail in their missions, but they usually knew they had failed!

Shortly afterwards he had to fly over to America himself and put the case over again. But the ground had been prepared, and the unexpected fall of Tobruk convinced the President that we must not fool about with "2nd" fronts now until we were secure in North Africa. We also accomplished one or two secondary tasks while in Washington, notably an agreement about a standard and uniform nomenclature for landing craft and landing ships.

Hitherto there had been no less than five separate systems in force. The American Bureau of Ships used one nomenclature, so also did the United States Marines, and the United States Navy. That made three systems. In addition, the Royal Navy and the Army also had their own names, making five systems in all. On the new system agreed at a meeting in Washington (at which, to my great surprise, Admiral Ernie King himself was present), we evolved a system which was admittedly ponderous, but which was at least self-evident and standardised.

I returned to England, as did so many Service Personnel at that time, in a "Liberator" bomber, and fortunately the flight was not attended by the intense cold from which so many passengers suffered. Among the passengers was a very youthful A.C.2, who was being flown home on compassionate grounds because his mother was ill. As we approached Prestwich Aerodrome, he told me in a lordly way that he had no doubt a special aircraft would be waiting to take him to Hendon, and would I like a passage.

Of course, I jumped at the chance, which saved much time and avoided the exhausting train journey in a crowded train. In exchange I gave him a lift in an Admiralty car sent to meet me, to Sloane Square where he lived. All ended happily because on arrival it appeared there had been a misunderstanding and Mum was perfectly fit and well.

Chapter 4

THE DIEPPE RAID

I had spent the first few days of June in Washington, having accompanied Mountbatten there in an attempt to convince the U.S. Administration that Britain was right in her refusal to undertake a major holding operation in France during 1942. Although we had two long meetings with the Combined Chiefs of Staff, followed by one between Mountbatten and the President himself, the Americans remained sceptical. But we had at least prepared the ground, and when Mr Churchill himself went over a little later, he finally persuaded Mr Roosevelt that such an operation would be folly.

I got back to London on 9 June 1942, and my first task was to tell the Members of the C.O.H.Q. Council the outcome of the talks in Washington. After that I devoted my time to joining the Camerons of Canada since I was determined to witness the Dieppe raid by landing with the battalion of that regiment who were taking part. This was not merely idle curiosity, although I was certainly interested to see what a raid looked like from a soldier's point of view.

The truth was that I had always been a little uneasy about planning hazardous operations backed by no personal experience and no sharing of the risks. But there is a difficulty about going as an "observer" in a warship if one happens to be a fairly senior Naval officer. The Naval Discipline Act does not recognise "observers", and, if one happens to be the Senior Officer present in a ship, one automatically bears responsibility for the manner in which she is handled and conducted. This is manifestly unfair on her Captain, and for practical purposes restricts one from proceeding as an observer unless the Naval Force Commander is your senior, and you travel in the ship in which he is flying his flag.

On the occasion of the raid on St. Nazaire, I had tried to watch what happened by going in one of the bombers. Unfortunately, the ground remained invisible, hidden by the tremendous thunder storm which synchronised with the raid. Apart, therefore, from spending a most alarming night, and gaining tremendous admiration for the courage of the bomber crews, who had to do this sort of thing night after night, I achieved nothing. Accordingly, I had approached General Roberts at a fairly early stage of the joint planning for Dieppe and secured his agreement to my landing with the Camerons. I chose that particular unit because it was the only battalion which was neither landing first nor coming off last. (I have never believed in talking undue risks!)

The General raised no objections, but stipulated that I must join the troops in time to take part in the rehearsal, and thus make sure that I was capable of keeping up with the battalion, who had some 7 miles to cover with full equipment during the course of the raid. He made the further condition that I must, of course, be guided by the instructions of the Security Authorities. These instructions were quite simple, and merely laid down that one must go as an "other rank" (because apparently the Germans never interrogated private soldiers), and that I must conform to whatever cover-story the Security people selected.

Accordingly, I proceeded at noon on 10 June to a flat in Artillery Mansions, which was occupied by a major of the Security Service. Here I was dressed up as a private soldier and taught how private soldiers spoke to corporals, and how they behaved in the presence of an officer, and so forth. I was also given bogus papers which had been prepared in the War Office. I then set forth to catch a train to the Isle of Wight and which was due to leave Victoria shortly after 13.00 hours. Praying inwardly that I should not come face to face with any friend or colleague as I strode down Victoria Street, I set forth.

Alas, my military career opened inauspiciously since I had not realised how very slippery the steel shod Army boots could be, with the result that I slipped and fell heavily after proceeding for only a few paces, and was helped to my feet by a kindly old lady. On arrival, in very good time at the station, I was directed into a special troop train which was still quite empty. The seats, I soon discovered, were too narrow to sit on with one's pack in position on one's back, and I did not dare to take it off as I was far from convinced that I should be able to strap it on again, so I stood in the corridor where I was joined by a friendly young man who had also just joined the Army, and who was equally afraid of taking off his pack. We agreed, however, that perhaps if we helped each other, we could get them on again, and we accordingly sat down in comfort until a very forceful lance corporal appeared and made us help with loading kit bags into the luggage van.

On arrival at Portsmouth Harbour Station, it transpired that the War Office had failed to provide me with the special pass which was required at that time by anybody who wishes to cross to the Isle of Wight. The Military Police did not, however, worry much about this, although I did experience some difficulty in landing at Ryde Pier, where an extremely alert and intelligent R.A.F. Corporal was in charge of the security arrangements. In due course a Canadian Army Jeep came and collected me, and drove me to a tented camp near Wootton Creek, where the Camerons were living at that time.

The thing that struck me most was the extreme informality of the Canadian Officers and N.C.O.s. For example, I was taken before the Adjutant once, who had been told to expect me as a clerical worker from C.O.H.Q. who was being lent to the Camerons for a period of infantry training. He assigned me to No.16 Platoon, and I was immediately led away to a tent which housed nine men of the Platoon. But these nine did not make up one complete section as might have been expected. On the contrary, the men had been arranged by age groups; the over 26s and the under 26s being kept separate. I was amused and flattered to find that I was lodged in an under 26s' tent, and I am bound to say I think I looked more like the younger age group than the older.

Most of the men came from the Winnipeg area. A number of them earning their living as hunters and trappers, and were aged by their tough life. They were naturally very fit and displayed a complete indifference to all outward forms of discipline. The Section Commanders were the key men. My own section was commanded by Lance Corporal Bender – a 22-year-old farmer for whom I quickly acquired a deep admiration and respect.

A typical day was to rise at 06.00 hours, breakfast at 06.30 hours, then take part in some form of physical exercise or unarmed combat until 09.00 hours. From 09.30 hours until 16.00 hours was devoted to an exercise, or "scheme", in the course of which we normally marched for about 16 miles.

On return to the camp, we rested and had tea and cleaned our weapons. Supper was at 19.00 hours, and was often followed by a lecture, during which one tried hard, and not always successfully, to keep awake. Then about 21.00 hours we had an unofficial meal which the Canadians called "lunch", and which normally consisted of one or two chickens stolen from a local farm and boiled in milk. After that we went to bed and slept the sleep of the just.

I remained with the Camerons until 21 June, and this period included the rehearsal for the raid which took place at Bridport, in West Bay. None of the battalion officers had apparently been briefed concerning the raid, and 20 June, the day on which it should have taken place, came and went with perfect weather, without anything happening at all. This was a contingency which I had not thought about. It was one thing to join the Camerons, but quite another matter to leave them and get clear of the Isle of Wight.

While I was wondering what to do on the evening of the 20th, I was summoned by a Corporal Clerk and escorted back to Ryde, whence I returned to London. After changing back into naval uniform, I went to C.O.H.Q. where I heard that the operation had been postponed for fourteen days, chiefly because General Paget considered the showing of the landing craft at the rehearsal had been below standard, and in this it appears he was right.

On Monday, 22 June, I accompanied Commodore Ellis to Broadlands where, after having tea with the Mountbattens, we drove to Portland and embarked in Mountbatten's official yacht *The Sister Anne*, which he used as a small H.Q. Ship. After dining on board, we sailed for Bridport to watch the second rehearsal the following morning. I myself landed with Generals Paget and Montgomery and we watched from the beach where the main landing was being simulated. In the course of this a Canadian soldier took careful aim and fired a smoke rocket at us. Monty took cover with great agility, but I made the mistake of supposing it would be easy to step aside as the rocket approached. Unfortunately, these rockets weave in their flights, and this one secured a direct hit on my shin, fortunately without breaking the bone.

Nevertheless, it was extremely painful, and I was grateful to accept the offer of a lift back to London in General Paget's special train. It was during this journey that Monty gave me a piece of personal advice in case I ever found myself directing a great battle, 'Such, for example,' he said, 'as will take place at Dieppe when the raid takes place. You will find that the Commander of a battle feels very lonely and gets a deep conviction that defeat is inevitable. That is the time', he went on, 'when great strength of mind is needed. All you must do', he insisted, 'is to trust the plan and let the battle win itself. The strength of mind required is simply to do nothing and refrain from dithering.' He went on to suggest that he would not be able to leave for Africa to supersede General Ritchie if only the General had let the battle in the desert win itself.

When the actual raid itself took place in August, I found that Monty had given similar advice to General Roberts, who unfortunately took it rather too literally.

After returning to London, I spent some busy days at C.O.H.Q., during which there were meetings galore on a number of abortive plans and operations, so much so that I felt at the time that our work was rapidly deteriorating into theoretical Whitehall planning, which is so costly in time, and so bad for morale.

Then on 30 June I went with Mountbatten to a meeting with the Prime Minister who wished to hold one final review of the outlook for the Dieppe raid and decide whether in the prevailing circumstances it was prudent to go on with it. The only other people present were General Ismay, Major General Hollis, the Secretary of the Chiefs of Staff's Committee, and Alanbrooke, the C.I.G.S. The meeting took place in the Cabinet Room, and oddly enough, Mrs Churchill was also present in the room. In the course of the discussion Mr Churchill suddenly turned to me and asked whether I could guarantee success! The C.I.G.S. interrupted and told me not to reply. 'If he, or anyone else, could guarantee success', he said, 'there would indeed be no object in doing the operation. It is just because no-one has the slightest idea what the outcome will be that the operation is necessary.'

Mr Churchill then said that this was not a moment at which he wanted to be taught adversity. 'In that case,' said Alanbrooke, 'you must abandon the idea of invading France because no responsible General will be associated with any planning for invasion until we have an operation at least of the size of the Dieppe raid behind us to study and base our plans upon'. Mr Churchill at once agreed that if that were Alanbrooke's considered view, we must go forward. He would ask Mr. Atlee to inform the War Cabinet, and he would inform the King.

On 2 July, I went in the evening to the Security Major's flat and got ready for an early start the following day, when I proceeded to Newhaven and re-joined the Camerons on board a Thames paddle steamer called *The Aristocrat*. In the afternoon of that day the troops were told for the first time about the operation, and there was great enthusiasm. They spent the evening studying maps which had been issued, and writing out their wills on special printed forms.

At about 20.00 hours we heard that the operation was again postponed. After another day on board *The Aristocrat*, D Company, to which No.16 Platoon belonged, was transferred to a larger Thames steamer called *The Royal Eagle*, where conditions were even more crowded because a battalion of French Canadians was also on board.

We remained on board until 7 July, during most of which time the ships were anchored off Newhaven in steadily deteriorating weather. On the evening of 7 July, to the intense disappointment of all troops, we were told that the operation had been laid off. I managed to get ashore, and, after spending the night in the naval guard room, I took an early morning train back to London.

Although my time with the Canadian troops failed to achieve its main object, I have never regretted it. In the first place it was a wonderful mental rest, and left me as fit as I have ever been in my life. It also taught me a tremendous amount about the domestic arrangements that must be made for troops embarked in landing craft for long periods. In particular, it is quite unreasonable to expect the Army to make the arrangements for feeding the troops. If their life is to be tolerable, all domestic details can much more easily be organised by the Navy.

This was one of the major changes that I was able to introduce when, a few weeks later, I was appointed in command of the Channel Assault Force. The outlook and attitude of the rank and file was also rather an eye-opener to me. The outstanding impression left by them on my mind was a friendly acceptance of strangers like myself, planted in their midst, coupled with a total lack of curiosity. Almost without exception, the younger men (and most of them were very young indeed) were extremely gregarious in the sense of hating to be alone, and always asking one to go with them for a walk, or visit the cinema, etc, etc., while also being almost entirely devoid of anything that could be called conversation.

Back in London on 8 July, we held a long inquest on the Dieppe operation at C.O.H.Q. in the course of which I demanded that there should be a formal enquiry. Nothing was decided at the time, and our attention was diverted by a strong rumour that General Marshall was about to be appointed as Supreme Commander in the U.K. and Channel area, with Mountbatten becoming his Chief of Staff. At the same time my own staff was strengthened by the addition of Commander (Now Rear Admiral) Elliott Strauss, U.S.N. I had known Strauss before the war when he was Assistant Naval Attaché, and it would be hard to imagine a more helpful officer, or one more calculated to ensure smooth relations with the American Naval Authorities.

About a week later I was sent down to Portsmouth to see the Naval Commander-in-Chief, Admiral Sir William James, to tell him that it had been virtually decided to re-mount the Dieppe raid with slight modifications to the plan, and carry it out on or about 18 August. This recommendation had been reached on 11 July at a meeting attended only by Mountbatten, Leigh-Mallory, General Roberts and myself. Nothing was put in writing, but General Ismay informed the Chiefs of Staff and the Prime Minister, who gave their verbal approval.

When I returned to London after seeing Admiral James, I found that it had also been provisionally decided that I was to be the Naval

Force Commander of the re-mounted operation, to which the code-name *Jubilee* had been assigned, and I received official confirmation on 20 July, in the form of a minute from the Chief of Staff's Committee.

Three weeks of intense work followed.

The main problem which faced us was security. After all, thousands of officers and men had been fully briefed with regard to the plan for the raid, and there was an obvious risk, to put it mildly, that some rumours about the plan would leak to the Germans.

Furthermore, the situation had changed in three ways since the operation had been dismounted early in July. In the first place, two additional assault ships had become available. One of them was the brand-new *Invicta*, built for the Dover/Boulogne run and the pride of the Southern Railway. Although she had never been to sea, there seemed to be no reason why she should not make her maiden trip with troops embarked for Dieppe.

By using these two ships we were able to carry sufficient troops by sea to substitute Commandos for parachute troops and thus eliminate one of the more complex timing problems that the operation involved. Secondly, the nights had lengthened sufficiently for it to be possible to carry out the operation on a single tide from 18 August onwards, provided the first landings were timed for the beginning of nautical twilight. (To the Landsman "nautical twilight", which starts when the sun is 12° below the horizon, is commonly regarded as darkness. "First light" is usually taken as the beginning of "civil twilight", which starts when the sun is 6° below the horizon.)

Thirdly, and most inconveniently, there was reason to think that the Germans had re-laid a minefield down the middle of the central Channel. Little was known about the density or efficiency of this minefield, but vessels could not approach the French coast between the Pas-de-Calais and the Baie de la Seine without crossing it, and it would have been quite irresponsible for us to ignore its existence. Obviously, we could not sweep and buoy wide approach channels through the minefield during daylight hours.

The best we could attempt would be to send mine-sweepers ahead of the raiding force to sweep, and, if possible, mark channels through which to pass. This, I could see, was going to be easier said than done. The Admiralty were able to make available two flotillas of ocean-going minesweepers, but no more. This would enable two channels, each a quarter of a mile wide, to be swept at a speed of approximately 8 knots. The nine destroyers and nine assault ships taking part in the operation would have to follow the sweepers through these channels as soon as they were cleared, at a speed of between 16 and 19 knots. There was no margin of time, or indeed, of sea room. The guiding ships of each group of assault ships must, therefore, hit off the north-westerly end of the narrow-swept channels with dead accuracy, and the question was how?

In March 1942, the R.A.F. had introduced the "Gee" system of radar navigation to help Bomber Command find its targets. It occurred to me to ask Sir Henry Tizard how accurate "G" was likely to be at surface height in the central Channel. Sir Henry's reply was encouraging. So, Commander Michael Hodges, the Chief Signal Officer at C.O.H.Q., was asked to approach the appropriate Naval Authorities with a view to getting receiving apparatus fitted in the senior officers' ships of minesweeping flotillas, and all assault ships and destroyers, that would be leaders for passing through the swept channel, and last, but not least, of my own designated Headquarter ship, H.M.S. *Calpe*. All this was done with astonishing speed and by the end of July, all the hardware was ready, although, whereas the R.A.F. called it "G", the Admiralty christened it the "QH" system.

There remained the tricky problem of securing the co-operation of the Commander-in-Chief, Bomber Command. Air Chief Marshal Harris had a reputation of being lukewarm in his enthusiasm towards operations other than strategic bombing! Leigh-Mallory strongly advised me to approach him direct, and I did so. At that time there were two chains of transmitting stations for "G" – the Southern and the Eastern. Only one could be switched on at a time depending on whether Bomber Command's target was to be in central or eastern Germany, or in France or the Rhineland.

What I had to ask, therefore, was that the Air Chief Marshal would operate on the southern chain on the night of the raid, and would also tell us on what dates the southern chain would be on during the first half of August. (This was necessary for purposes of practice and test). In addition, we needed to be told what corrections had to be applied on each of the days when we should be using our "QH". This was rather a tall order for so busy a man as "Bomber Harris", especially in view of the importance he attached to preserving secrecy with regard to future objectives of his aircraft.

In the event, the Air Chief Marshal proved more than friendly and helpful. We practised every group leader between 5 and 15 August, going to sea on five or six nights for the purpose. The results gave us every confidence in the accuracy of this new navigational aid. By a piece of luck, as we subsequently discovered, the "G" system was exceptionally accurate at the positions where the swept channels were established. Further to the East and West it became progressively less accurate and would not have done for the particular purpose for which we required to use it.

By far my greatest anxiety, however, was over security. Yet, I felt myself, that we could still achieve surprise if we could be sure that the enemy remained unaware that we were getting ready again for any combined operation at all. There must, therefore, be no further rehearsals of the landings which could be observed and photographed from the air. Fortunately, General Roberts required no more. There must be no great assembly of landing ships and landing craft in the Solent, such as had preceded the earlier attempt in July and had been observed and attacked by enemy aircraft. Fortunately, all the ships and craft we needed were still in the Portsmouth/Southampton/Newhaven areas and all the Army units were within an hour's bus drive of them. Thus, no tell-tale movements of ships and craft were needed until dusk on the evening before the landings.

It is normal practice before a big operation to call in the security people who advise on a "cover plan". This assumes that the enemy will be aware of the troop and ship concentrations that have to be made, and the cover plan is intended to mislead him about their purpose. On this occasion I decided against having a cover plan, because the object was to conceal any hint of an unusual concentration of ships and craft. This being so, a cover plan would have been a two-edged weapon against us; it would have invited the enemy's attention to things that we hoped he would not have observed at all, and it might not have proved easy to deceive him about their true significance.

Moreover, it certainly would not have been possible to deceive our own Commanding Officers, and if you do not take them into your confidence, they will not be inhibited from speculating and before long the secret becomes an open one so far as the forces taking part are concerned. This was one of the lessons I learned from our futile operations in Norway in 1940, and I had never forgotten it.

Accordingly, we did not call in the security people before Dieppe, but each Force Commander interviewed every Captain and Commanding Officer separately and alone. We told them exactly what was intended and instructed each to invent his own story – for the benefit of his own officers and men (to account for his own particular ship or battalion remaining where it was during the first half of August instead of returning to its normal base). This was done during the last week of July. A special difficulty arose, however, over the Combined Signal Unit, comprising over 100 men from all three Services which had to be especially re-assembled, and whose members could not so easily be fobbed off.

My Signal Officer was Lieutenant Peter Howes, R.N., who afterwards rose to be Flag Officer Middle East. He handled the problem with imagination and success. A sizeable country house near Aldershot, already under requisition by the War Office, was borrowed on an "old boy" basis, and the men of the Combined Unit were housed there, and exercised in the Home Park from the end of July until the day on which the Force sailed. The local villages were told that these men were the survivors from a torpedoed troop ship.

The men themselves were told what the villagers had been told, and also that the true reason for getting them together was that His Majesty The King had expressed a desire to see a large combined operation demonstration before the end of August; that the only thing that could be laid on quickly was a repeat of the rehearsal for Dieppe, such as they had already done twice at Bridport, but they were warned to keep this very secret since if the enemy got to know, His Majesty's safety, and indeed their own safety, might be endangered by fighter bomber attacks on the beaches. As things turned out, complete secrecy was preserved.

Although the enemy had known for weeks that we had on the south coast the potential to carry out a large raid, and although they had seen and attacked the assembly of ships in July, the German records show that their High Command had no inkling that anything was planned or mounted in August. On the contrary, Marshal von Rundstedt relaxed the degree of preparedness which had been in force in June and July, and the Luftwaffe Commander in the Dieppe area actually granted extended night leave until noon on the very day that the raid took place! Unfortunately for us, the Major General Commanding the Dieppe Garrison had countermanded von Rundstedt's relaxation – not because he had fore-knowledge, but because he felt it was premature to relax so long as the weather and tidal conditions remained favourable to raiding operations.

It could therefore be said, although I do not think it ever has been said, except by myself in my despatch, that one lesson of the Dieppe raid was that contrary to all probability, it was still possible to achieve tactical surprise in a considerable cross-Channel operation provided one went about it the right way.

We made one other change in the revised plan inasmuch as I have mentioned before, we substituted two Commando landings for parachute troops to take care of the two heavy coastal batteries at Berneval and Varengeville-sur-Mer. Leigh-Mallory was against the use of airborne troops in principle because of the timing difficulties that always arose if they are used. The Commandos chosen were No.3

under Brigadier Durnford-Slater's command and No.4 under Lord Lovatt's command. The latter were to attack the battery south-west of Dieppe and to make their passage in the assault ship *Prince Albert*, while Durnford-Slater's Commando crossed in L.C.(P) from Newhaven, being escorted by coastal craft and L.C.F. (No.1), which carried an armament of four 4" guns. Collectively these craft were called No.5 Group, the Naval Commander being Commander Derek Wyburd.

On the day before the raid, I wrote two important letters to Mountbatten, with copies of each to the Commander-in-Chief, Portsmouth, and to Leigh-Mallory and General Roberts. In one of these letters, I placed on record my opinion that the Navy must never again rely upon ad-hoc forces specially assembled to carry out operations of the size and complexity of the Dieppe raid. The reliance on ships and craft supplied by functional commands, such as Coastal Forces or the Combined Operations Command, involves a separation of administrative command from operational command. There may be occasions when this is unavoidable, but it is always undesirable. Two examples of what can happen, and indeed what did happen, during the few days before the Dieppe raid well illustrate the point.

All the Tank Landing Craft allocated to me for the Operation came under the administrative Command of the "Captain L.C.T.", whose headquarters were established at Troon. During the period before the operation, those required to take part were berthed mainly at Southampton, where the Captain L.C.T. had established a temporary base for them. One of the flotillas had to sail from Newhaven in order to arrive at Dieppe at the same time as the first main landings. But there was a difficulty inasmuch as the loading hards at Newhaven were not strong enough to take the weight of Churchill tanks, which meant that the nearest place to Newhaven at which this flotilla could embark its tanks was Stokes Bay in the Solent.

Obviously, we could not risk loading the flotilla the day before the raid and sending it round to Newhaven, as such a movement could hardly fail to be observed by Air Reconnaissance. Accordingly, we sent the flotilla with its craft empty to Newhaven about a fortnight before the raid was due to take place in order to get the Germans used to seeing some tank landing craft lying at Newhaven.

During the week or so before the raid we brought the tank landing craft back to the Solent in pairs, embarked their tanks during the night, and sailed them back to Newhaven immediately afterwards. We did not think that a trickle movement of this sort would attract the enemy's attention, and it was a great relief when, two days before the raid, all the craft were correctly loaded and assembled, and our Intelligence told us that there were no indications that German suspicions had been aroused.

The following day, that is to say the day before the raid, I was astounded to learn that the entire flotilla had returned to Southampton. On making enquiries I learned that this move had been ordered from Troon, partly to facilitate the fortnightly payments of the crews, and partly because all the First Lieutenants and half the Commanding Officers were due for relief and were in fact relieved by orders from Troon the day before the operation! Needless to say, the Captain L.C.T. himself had no knowledge of the operation, and all security would have been lost had we been obliged to send details of what was intended to numerous bases and commanding officers who administered the huge Combined Operations Command.

The other incident was not dissimilar. I had obtained the use of, I think, two flotillas of obsolescent motor gunboats which had an unusually large smoke-laying capability. Their prime role in the operation was to make smoke when necessary to protect landing craft lying offshore from the enemy fire. These craft were administered by the Captain of H.M.S. *Hornet* which was the principal Coastal Craft base in the country.

Fortunately, the Senior Officer of the gunboats was a young man of common sense, and he came up to Fort Southwick 48 hours before the raid to tell me that he had just received orders from the Captain of H.M.S. *Hornet* to return there at once so that the smoke making apparatus could be dismantled and removed!

I therefore urged in my letter that if we really intended to invade France later in the war, we should lose no time in creating a composite force of sufficient landing craft and ships to lift, say, a Brigade Group organised and deployed for an initial assault. This force should have its own escort craft and destroyers, its own navigational craft to act as guides to landing craft flotillas, and its own Headquarters Ship. The primary role of the force should be training, and it should be expanded steadily as the date for the invasion approached until it was large enough to lift the whole of the British Army Units which were to be committed to the assault. A secondary role would be to carry out cross-Channel raids from time to time as opportunity offered. Above all, this Naval Assault Force should be commanded through the normal naval chain of command.

My other letter, which was concerned only with the Dieppe raid, set forth in detail the losses of ships or landing craft which we might suffer on passage and which would lead me to abandon the operation and turn back, as opposed to those losses which I felt we could accept

Troops of a US Ranger battalion training in the United Kingdom having been attached to Combined Operations. The Rangers are training under commando instructors and undergoing an opposed landing exercise with British naval instructors. (NARA)

Royal Navy sailors at work destroying mining explosives at Ny-Ålesund during Operation *Gauntlet*, the Combined Operations raid on the Svalbard archipelago that began on 19 August 1941. The aims of the attack were the destruction or removal of the various coal mining facilities, any stocks of coal, the transport facilities between mines and wharves, any harbour facilities, and the wireless and meteorological stations. (National Museum of the US Navy)

Commandos in action during Operation *Archery*, the Combined Operations raid on Vågsøy and Måløy, Norway, which was undertaken on 27 December 1941.

A badly wounded raider is assisted back to a landing craft during Operation *Archery*, the raid on Vågsøy and Måløy on 27 December 1941.

The radar station on the cliff top at Bruneval, which was the main target of Operation *Biting*, the Combined Operations attack undertaken on the night of 27–28 February 1942. Using screwdrivers, crowbars and brute force, the raiders ripped out or dismantled every important component of the radar station. With the task completed, the force began to withdraw to the beach, from where they were successfully uplifted by the Royal Navy.

German prisoners being searched on one of the vessels returning from Operation *Biting*. The original caption notes that the 'prisoner on the right is a member of the Luftwaffe; the other is an infantryman. The paratroop's second rifle was taken from the Germans.'

Major Lord Lovat pictured giving orders to his men before setting out on Operation *Abercrombie*. This was an Anglo-Canadian reconnaissance raid on the area around the French coastal village of Hardelot, located to the south of Boulogne-sur-Mer. The raid went ahead on the night of 21–22 April 1942.

Men of No.4 Commando pictured after their return from Operation *Abercrombie*, 22 April 1942. The raid was the first time that examples of the newly introduced Landing Ship Supports were used.

Combined Operations training underway in the UK. In this case, troops are undergoing a final training exercise prior to the attack on Dieppe, Operation *Jubilee*, which was carried out on 19 August 1942. (Courtesy of Library and Archives Canada)

Canadian troops disembarking from landing craft during training exercises on the south coast before the raid on Dieppe in August 1942. (Courtesy of Library and Archives Canada)

Soldiers look out at the harbour at Dieppe as their landing craft makes its way towards the beach at the start of Operation *Jubilee*, 19 August 1942.

A scene of death and destruction on the beach at Dieppe that was taken after the Allied withdrawal on 19 August 1942. Here a German soldier can be seen picking his way through abandoned equipment and the bodies of some of the fallen.

Training for D-Day. Utilising all the experience gained from Combined Operations' previous attacks and raids, here US troops are pictured landing on a beach in the UK during a rehearsal for the Normandy landings. (NARA)

Troops crouch inside a Landing Craft Vehicle Personnel, or LCVP, just before landing on Omaha Beach on D-Day, 6 June 1944. (USNHHC)

Commandos of 47 (RM) Commando coming ashore from LCAs on Jig Green Beach, Gold area, on 6 June 1944. LCTs unloading priority vehicles of 231st Brigade, 50th Division, can be seen in the background. (© MoD/Crown Copyright 2019)

Following his time in Combined Operations, Vice Admiral Hughes-Hallett returned to sea, being made captain of the Fiji-class light cruiser HMS *Jamaica*.

and ignore. Naturally this letter was prepared in close consultation with General Roberts, and it gave the reasons which lay behind our thinking. A decision to abandon a Combined Operation whilst still at sea must be a joint one, but the executive action which has to be taken is purely Naval, is usually irreversible, and therefore needs to be decided upon in advance because there may be no time for consultation when the crisis comes.

With these letters done, we held a short Force Commanders Meeting on Sunday, 16 August, and decided to postpone the operation for 24 hours on account of a poor weather forecast. On 17 August, David Luce and I spent the forenoon going very carefully through Operation Orders, while in the afternoon we took a three-hour walk, and went over the whole operation in our minds trying to imagine and anticipate all the contingencies that might arise.

On Tuesday, 18 August, I went for a short run on the Portsdown Hills before breakfast, as was my custom, and then made final preparations for sailing. In the afternoon I slept until 16.00 hours, when we held a meeting at Fort Southwick, which was attended by the three Force Commanders, by Admiral Sir William James, and by Mountbatten. Despite a more than doubtful weather forecast, Leigh-Mallory and I pressed hard for a decision to sail that evening, and this was agreed.

We were influenced by Lieutenant Ronald Bell, who at that time was the Meteorological Officer at the Fleet Air Arm base at Lee-on-Solent, and since the war has sat in the Commons for many years as Member for South Buckinghamshire. Ronnie Bell had expert local weather knowledge, and he predicted a pocket of fine weather in the central Channel area that would last until the late afternoon of 19 August. In this prediction he was alone, because both the Admiralty and the Air Ministry Weather Experts were every bit as gloomy as the Old Testament Prophets. Indeed, the last message I received before leaving Fort Southwick by car at 19.30 hours was from the Admiralty Director of Operations begging me not to sail that evening on account of the weather.

However, the die was cast, and the General and I, with our respective Staffs, embarked on H.M.S. *Calpe* at 19.45 hours on 18 August and sailed at 20.00 hours. It was a perfect evening and the *Calpe* stopped at the gate through the Spithead Anti-Submarine Room and watched as the whole force passed through, eastward bound, in perfect formation and dead on time.

Meanwhile, Mountbatten returned with Leigh-Mallory to No.11 Group's headquarters at Uxbridge, where he could keep in constant touch with events at sea and off Dieppe.

Mr Quentin Reynolds, the well-known American journalist and broadcaster was on board as an observer, and I remember his asking me what the responsibility felt like. It was in fact my first time afloat in Command in the rank of Captain, and David Luce's first trip to sea in the rank of Commander. We both agreed at the time that the experience of watching literally hundreds of ships and craft as far as the eye could see wherever we looked, and knowing that all were under our command and committed to the greatest amphibious operation since Gallipoli, had a certain dream-like quality.

Once all the main units were clear of the gate, the *Calpe* increased to full speed and proceeded to take the van. We then reduced to 18 knots and steered for the south-westerly of the two swept channels. I felt a deep sense of relief that at least the entire Force was safely at sea, and without apparently having been detected – all this despite the foreboding of some of the Naval Staff at Portsmouth, who had confidently predicted that so big a Force would never even clear the gate. I then lay down in the Captain's sea cabin and rested, reflecting that perhaps the most remarkable thing about the operation was that it had actually been launched and despite so much obstruction and so much frustration that had dogged Combined Operations since early April 1942.

Looking back after thirty years I still consider that the most remarkable thing about the Dieppe raid was that it did in fact take place, and for this the chief credit must go to the constancy of purpose of the Prime Minister, Mountbatten, Leigh-Mallory and General Roberts.

One great difficulty with which we all had to contend was the immense complexity of the Operation Order, which each Service found it necessary to issue. At the time of Dieppe there was no set pattern for such orders, but guided mainly by Leigh-Mallory, with his own unrivalled operational experience, we felt our way forward to what was destined to become standard practice. We first produced what we called "a combined plan".

This plan was signed jointly by the three Force Commanders and formally approved by Mountbatten as Chief of Combined Operations. It included a chronological timetable which showed in tabular form exactly what each unit in each Service ought to be doing, and where it should be from minute to minute throughout the operation. The Combined Plan was not an "Order", but it enabled each Force Commander to issue Operation Orders to give effect to the plan. These Operation Orders were widely criticised on this occasion for being too complicated.

The German High Command who captured a copy of the Army Operation Orders subsequently condemned them for being unduly rigid and detailed. Perhaps they were? But they were being issued to very raw troops. Similarly, my own Naval Operation Orders were far longer than would have been necessary, had one been dealing with a Force that had worked together before, and which was guided by standard "Fighting Instructions", as in the case of the Fleet.

One of the first things I did after the raid was to draw up a body of Fighting Instructions to govern the conduct of a Naval Assault Force when carrying out amphibious operations. But at the time of Dieppe, it was as if, when issuing Operation Orders to a Fleet one had to write, for example: 'The Fleet will weigh anchor at 0600, and leave Harbour by the western entrance. (Instructions for weighing anchor, and for passage through the western entrance are to be found in appendices 1 & 2 respectively).'

By the end of 1943 we found it possible to operate much larger Forces of Landing Craft with much shorter Orders.

On the whole, the passage to Dieppe was carried out accurately and according to plan. It is true that the *Queen Emma* inadvertently led her group through the wrong swept channel in which she overtook a flotilla of Tank Landing Craft and some other small vessels for which it was reserved. Fortunately, this caused no mishap and no delay. After the Assault Ships had lowered their landing craft, and while they were forming up to return to England, the *Invicta* and the *Princess Beatrix* were in collision. Both ships were extensively damaged, but reached Southampton without difficulty. These alarums did not disturb me, as strict wireless silence was maintained and I was able to sleep peacefully until 03.00 hours: the time at which the Assault Ships stopped to lower their boats.

I then went on the bridge, while the *Calpe* remained stopped about 12 miles off the main beaches, and waited for the Landing Craft from the Assault Ships to complete about half their run inshore before following them in. It was while we were stopped that we saw gunfire away to the north-eastward at about 03.50 hours, which we judged to originate from an action between No.5 Group (i.e., the craft carrying No.3 Commando together with their escort,) and enemy coastal craft. Actually, they were in action with a small German coastal convoy. I have read in accounts of the raid about the agonising decision that then faced me on whether to call off the whole operation at this moment. But, of course, the decision had already been made and committed to paper in the letter I have already referred to.

It would, moreover, have been difficult to call off the operation once the Landing Craft were proceeding towards their beaches in large numbers. Besides, I thought it unlikely that the Germans would have associated what must have looked to them like a Coastal Force Skirmish, with a major combined operation. In England such an incident would have alerted our Coast Defence Batteries, but not infantry garrisons; and this is precisely what happened on this occasion.

I was, however, somewhat surprised at receiving no report from Commander Wyburd, since he would have been justified in breaking wireless silence once his group was in action. But no message came because, as later transpired, his wireless was put out of action almost by the first shot. This chance encounter was unfortunate inasmuch as the landing craft were dispersed, and No.3 Commando was in consequence easily repulsed, with heavy losses when it eventually landed. However, the failure of the attack on the battery at Berneval had no material effect on the operation as a whole. That this was so was largely thanks to the persistence, skill, and courage, of Captain Peter Young[1] and a handful of soldiers who landed unopposed and got within 200 yards of the battery, which they successfully sniped from the cover of a cornfield, until 09.00 hours. Although the gunners trained their guns inland, and opened fire on Captain Young at point blank range, they could not depress the guns sufficiently, and the shells whistled over their heads, causing no casualties.

From the Naval point of view the least successful landing was that of the assault landing craft carrying the Royal Regiment of Canada, whose task was to land at Puits, and storm the vital cliffs which dominated the town and the beaches from the north-east side. This group of landing craft were beached some fifteen to twenty minutes late because of confusion while forming up. They also ran in so fast that their approach was heard and seen by the enemy.

Yet the main landings at Dieppe were made with greater accuracy in time and position than had ever been achieved, or was destined to be achieved again. Indeed, the first waves of landing craft on the two beaches came in within two minutes of the scheduled time, and within seconds of the Fighter Bomber attack which was put in just before the craft were due to beach. The flotilla of tank landing craft which had orders to land its tanks "with, but after" the infantry, landed twenty-eight out of thirty Churchill tanks some nine minutes after the troops.

---

1 Brigadier Peter Young afterwards became a military historian of distinction and a lecturer at Sandhurst.

By the time these landings took place, the *Calpe* had followed in to less than 3 miles from the beaches, so we had a grandstand view, and not even in exercises have I witnessed such precision. Neither, at first, did there seem to be much opposition, but opposition grew with disastrous speed once the troops were ashore, thus making it impossible to observe progress being made. Nevertheless, I felt sure that things were going badly, partly through the sight of so many damaged landing craft limping back through the smoke and making for the "boat pool", which had been established 4 miles out to sea, and partly because the reports being received by General Roberts in his improvised Operations Room below the bridge, were chaotic and uninformative.

In contrast, the reports from the landings at Pourville were more cheerful, and we soon learned that Pourville itself had fallen and that the Canadians were advancing inland. Similarly, Lord Lovat's Commando achieved complete success in their attack on Varengeville-sur-Mer Battery, which was swiftly captured and destroyed: "a copy book operation" was how I described it at the time, and no subsequent information has altered that assessment.

Why did the troops, who landed so easily at first on the main beaches, fail to exploit their initial success and get pinned down and massacred? Why were the captors of Pourville unable to reach their objectives, or indeed to hold the high ground which dominated the beach on which they had landed, and from which they had to withdraw? Much has been written about this, and it is not for me – a professional sailor – to adjudicate. It was certainly through no lack of courage or determination, although Dieppe did show once again that valour, however matchless it may be, is not by itself enough: battle experience and the right sort of equipment are also needed. All I can do is to set forth some of the factors which led to the repulse with fearful loss of the 2nd Canadian Division.

Firstly, the enemy were in greater strength than we had been led to expect. I have seen it stated that there were no less than four times as many troops in the area as had been estimated in the intelligence on which Monty had based his original outline plan. Secondly, neither Leigh-Mallory nor I had any effective means of supporting the troops once they were ashore, although Mountbatten at Uxbridge did his utmost to urge Leigh-Mallory to send in more bombers, yet the Air Marshal could do little. This was not solely through lack of suitable Bomber aircraft, for which we had vainly pressed, it was also due to the inability of the troops to tell us accurately where they were, or what targets they wanted destroyed.

In contrast, Lord Lovat had defined the precise line he intended to reach, and where he would halt his troops before putting in his final assault on the battery. He had also told Leigh-Mallory the exact time at which his troops would move into the attack. This made it possible for the Air Marshal to lay on an effective bomber attack at the time and place it was needed. But although Leigh-Mallory had pressed for similar information from the Canadians, General Roberts felt unable to give it because, he urged, his troops must press on as and when they could.

Another great handicap was the presence in the tank landing craft of hundreds of specialised troops – notably demolition engineers – with heavy loads of explosives and other equipment to carry ashore. When the moment came, they were confronted with murderous machine-gun fire, and the craft themselves, while waiting for these men to land, became the target for an ever-growing volume of cannon fire. Indeed, the flotilla of Mark II Landing Craft Tank which had landed with the first wave of troops, were destined to suffer casualties amounting to 50% of their personnel. Most of the craft were eventually either sunk or severely damaged, and so far as could be made out, nearly all the damage and casualties occurred after the tanks had got safely ashore and while the craft were waiting for the specialised troops to land.

Similarly, I learned for the first time some twenty-five years after the raid, that the infantry who landed in the first wave of the assault had been hampered by the number of "Observers" and "Special Parties" who had infiltrated into the units who were to be first ashore in the assault. On the Naval side, we had received innumerable requests of this nature, which was indeed inevitable at that stage of the war when Whitehall was teeming with gallant and enthusiastic young officers whose supreme ambition was to see action. But David Luce had been adamant in his opposition to having either the ships or the landing craft cluttered up with people who were not directly concerned with the operation itself.

At Pourville, the failure of the infantry to reach their inland objectives was mainly due to the fact that they were not supported by tanks, as had been hoped. The Beach-Master in this area – Commander Redvers Prior, R.N. – had signalled to me that reconnaissance after the landings had revealed too flat a shallow gradient offshore, which would render the passage of tank landing craft to the beaches impossible. Since Commander Prior was a particularly experienced and reliable officer, I had no hesitation in diverting this group of tank landing craft to a waiting position off the main beaches in the hope that they could land their tanks at the south-west end of the Dieppe seafront, and approach

Pourville from the East. However, the failure to secure these beaches made this impracticable.

Deprived as they were of their armour, the Camerons of Canada did very well to get as far inland as they did. But of all the shortcomings and misfortunes which contributed to the awful losses suffered by the Canadian division, the one that mattered most, and that determined the course of the battle, was the total failure of the landing at Puits and the consequential failure to capture high ground and fortified cliffs which dominated the harbour and town from the East. In the original plan it had been intended that Captain Ryder, V.C. in H.M.S. *Locust*, should lead the Free French Chasseurs into the harbour at about 07.00 hours, and that once inside, the Chasseurs, in whom were embarked one of the Marine Commandos, should land the troops on the quay where they would take the Germans defending the main beaches in the rear.

When I realised from a verbal report from Lieutenant Commander Colin McMullen (who had led in some of the landing craft carrying the Royal Regiment) that there was no prospect of the east cliffs being captured, I doubted whether Ryder's mission was feasible. Accordingly, I signalled him to repair on board the *Calpe*, which he did at about 06.30 hours.

With great moral courage he told me that he felt certain that any attempt to enter the harbour would be attended by the loss of all the ships concerned, since they would have to run the gauntlet at point blank range of batteries of medium calibre guns concealed in caves dug into the side of the cliffs. Reluctantly, therefore, with General Roberts' full agreement, I cancelled the *Locust*'s mission, and had the Royal Marine Commando transferred to assault landing craft which, at the General's request, were sent in to reinforce his hard-pressed troops on the main beaches. It was, of course, a mistake on the part of the General to reinforce failure. The Marines who got ashore lost heavily for nothing gained, whereas had they been landed at Pourville they might have achieved something.

All this time the *Calpe* continued to lie about 2 miles offshore, remaining stopped most of the time, but shifting her position at intervals when gaps in the drifting smoke brought her under heavy fire from the shore.

As always, the smoke was a two-edged weapon. A light onshore wind carried it inland and obscured our view of what was happening on the beaches. On the other hand, it allowed us to remain in position where we could intercept landing craft returning from the shore towards the Boat Pool and thus obtain verbal reports on the situation ashore.

In addition, a number of officers in command of detached groups came alongside and reported to me on the bridge.

The first of these were Derek Wyburd and Durnford-Slater, both bleeding profusely from head wounds, who arrived at about 06.00 hours and told me the fate of No.5 Group. Later came McMullen, from whom I learned of the catastrophe at Puits. David Beatty, in command of the tank landing craft, also came to report of their achievements and losses, although at that time he did not realise the full extent of the damage and casualties they had suffered. One thing that still stands out in my memory is the spirit of exultation – almost a joy of battle – which a few officers and some of the young ratings displayed amidst the din and carnage. Colin McMullen, Lord Beaty and Lieutenant Commander Wallace (the Captain of the *Calpe*) come particularly to my mind in this context.

Although we received no clear or authoritative reports from the troops ashore, I had no doubt of the gravity of their position. All that we gleaned from returning landing craft confirmed that the Canadians were pinned down on the beaches, and I felt sure that my own picture of the general situation – confused though it was – was a good deal clearer than that of General Roberts, who had nothing but a mass of garbled corrupt radio messages to go upon.

Accordingly, after talking it over with David Luce, I went down to the operations room at about 09.30 hours and advised the General to advance the time of withdrawal by thirty minutes or one hour, because I felt that with every minute's delay the difficulties of getting soldiers off alive would grow. I also urged that the amended Orders should be broadcast in an enciphered message, because we were already aware that the enemy were listening-in to the Canadian plain language radio traffic. However, the General told me that it was already too late for him to advance the time of withdrawal, which must remain as planned at 11.00 hours.

Even this presented some difficulty because the original orders provided for all the troops to be brought off from the main beaches on the Dieppe sea-front, and also for the main body to embark in tank landing craft with the assault landing craft being used only for the rear guard. The failure to capture Dieppe and the domination of all the beaches by enemy fire meant firstly, that the troops could only hope to get off from roughly where they had been landed, and secondly, that the only craft which could be sent in for them were armoured assault landing craft. I therefore signalled to Captain McLintock to repair on board *Calpe* and asked him to proceed to the Boat Pool, and explain verbally what the craft would have to do to bring the troops off;

undamaged tank landing craft were to be told to wait 2 miles offshore during the withdrawal, and to be prepared to receive wounded men who might be transferred to them by L.C.A. on their way back to England.

But the first thing was to cover the L.C.A. on their way into the beaches and to try to ensure that they touched down simultaneously and in good formation. A coded signal was made to all destroyers, landing craft flak, motor gun boats and steam gun boats, and also to those M.L.s which had acted as guides to L.C.A. in the early morning, ordering them to form a line of bearing parallel to the run of the coast between Puits and Pourville. This manoeuvre was surprisingly well executed and the whole force ran in under cover of renewed fire from destroyers and landing craft flak, and of smoke made by all the ships and craft able to make it. The wind carried the smoke screen ahead of the landing craft flotillas, which consequently came under little fire until they were close inshore.

H.M.S. *Calpe* closed the shore at the western end of the Pourville beach. Although this beach was hidden by smoke, the high ground to the west of it was visible above the smoke screen and the ship came under fairly heavy rifle fire before she stopped. However, no casualties were reported from this cause. Once the landing craft were beached and once the troops endeavoured to re-embark, they came under heavy murderous fire, and I doubt whether a withdrawal has ever been attempted under such terrible conditions, or whether greater sustained heroism has ever been displayed. In many cases landing craft sank as they went astern because they could not raise their ramps on account of the dead bodies which had piled up on them. The general conduct of the landing craft was beyond praise, and spoke volumes for the training they had received at their Scottish bases.

Although I could not see what was happening on the beaches themselves, it was possible to form an opinion of the progress of the withdrawal by watching the diminishing stream of L.C.A. proceeding past *Calpe* on their way seaward. A number of them came alongside and gave us news, and at the same time transferred the more seriously wounded men to the ship. It had originally been intended that all military wounded should be landed at Newhaven, where arrangements for their reception had been made. Yet it was impossible to refuse to receive them on board the destroyers, and, by the time we started the return journey some 550 badly wounded Canadians were on board the destroyers, while *Calpe* herself had embarked over 250 in addition to having suffered over 25% casualties among her own crew.

The beaches about which I knew least were the two main beaches, and finally, round about 13.00 hours, I asked Wallace to take the ship back through the smoke and have a final look. At the same time, we decided to open fire with the ship's main armament – since the radio equipment seemed by now to be of secondary importance. During this run-in we took with us two undamaged landing craft, stationed close enough to communicate with by megaphone, in case we should see small parties who might still be brought off.

As soon as we were through the smoke several things happened at once. *Calpe* came under very heavy fire from guns whose projectiles threw up vicious little water spouts all around the ship. I learned afterwards from the Army Officers on board that these projectiles were old fashioned shrapnel. The sound of *Calpe*'s 4" guns firing back cheered up all who were on board, especially as the return fire was effective and destroyed some of the pillboxes from which light automatic guns were firing.

The ship was eventually stopped slightly under a mile from the beaches, but no Canadian troops could be made out. Suddenly we saw a fighter approaching and a Sub-Lieutenant shouted to the gun layer of an Oerlikon just below our bridge, to open fire. A more senior officer told the gun-layer to wait until we were sure that the fighter was German, since we had already seen two Spitfires shot down by British fire. At this moment the leading edge of the fighter's wing appeared to turn blue and became incandescent.

A stream of canon shell followed, and we all dived for cover with as much dignity as we could. Most of the officers and men on the *Calpe*'s over-crowded bridge received superficial wounds, and as we stood up again, we presented a gory sight. Fortunately, David Luce, Lieutenant Commander Adrian Butler (my Navigating Officer), Peter Howes, and Wallace himself were untouched, and I was only cut on the nose and elbow. But below us in the wheel house, most of the occupants were killed and Ranald Boyle, my Personal Assistant, was severely wounded in the head. (However, he came to again later, and completed the note he was writing describing everything he saw. The notebook, stained with his blood, is now in the Maritime Museum.)

At about the same time, H.M.S. *Berkeley*, who was lying perhaps half a mile off the beach and very close to us, was hit by a heavy bomb. Some observers said that it had been jettisoned by a bomber that was about to crash. The ship was mortally damaged, and one could see her deck undulating in the gentle swell, indicating that her back was broken. Two or three coastal craft were alongside her within seconds, and she was abandoned with lightning speed. I ordered H.M.S. *Albrighton* to torpedo her, as we could not risk her drifting ashore and falling into enemy hands. When the torpedo hit, she blew up with a tremendous explosion. At much the same time, General Roberts appeared on the bridge and told me that the remaining troops on the main beaches had surrendered.

Slowly, we turned seaward and shaped course for Newhaven at the best speed of the crippled landing craft, which was under 4 knots.

The mass of the small landing craft were formed into an amorphous bunch surrounded by the larger craft armed with Oerlikons or better, while outside them there was a circle of destroyers. The whole formation was tantamount to a slowly moving Zareba, and it was noticeable that enemy aircraft seemed reluctant to press home attacks in the face of what added up to a formidable volume of anti-aircraft fire.

Up to this point the *Calpe* had not been seriously damaged, although casualties to personnel had been heavy and her upper deck was choked with seriously wounded soldiers. I recall a young ship's officer asking me whether I had ever believed the history books when they spoke of the "scuppers" running with blood. 'If not, lean over the bridge and take a look along the ship's side,' he added quietly. I did so and as the ship rolled very gently in a long, lazy swell, you could see little red rivulets running down out of each scupper.

It was at this stage that a very young fighter pilot who was on board to help the well-known Wing Commander Sprett with visual fighter direction, told me that one of our fighters was "ditching" about 10 miles to the north-west, and could we rescue the pilot. I hoisted the "Disregard"[2] and told H.M.S. *Fernie* to assume "Guide of the Fleet", and I then asked Wallace to increase to full speed and pick up the pilot. Wallace quite properly protested that this would hazard his ship. In this he was strongly backed by David Luce, who maintained at that moment we were clear of the Zareba we would become the target for every bomber in sight. This is just what did happen, and dive bombers delivered an effective attack before we were 5 miles clear of the main body.

There were several near misses which damaged *Calpe*'s hull and her steering gear. The ready use ammunition for the centre gun was set on fire and several seamen, whose clothing had caught fire, jumped overboard. They were rescued by Peter Scott in his steam gun boat. We re-joined the main body having apparently achieved nothing, yet in truth we had achieved a great deal.

---

2   i.e., A blue burgee, which signals that the Admiral's movements are to be disregarded.

Every intense battle involving both ships and aircraft was apt to leave an aftermath of bitterness. This stemmed from the extreme difficulty of distinguishing between friend and foe. Dieppe was no exception, and a total of six British aircraft were shot down by the A.A. guns of ships and landing craft. It was no consolation to Fighter Command Pilots to tell them that this figure compared favourably with previous experience, and was indeed destined to compare even more favourably with what happened in some of the great combined operations later in the war. But the risk taken by H.M.S. *Calpe* in her attempt to save this one pilot, and the damage and casualties which she suffered, came to be known, and helped to found a deep and enduring friendship and mutual trust between No.11 Group of Fighter Command and Force "J" as the naval survivors of the Dieppe raid came to be called. I cannot pretend that these thoughts were uppermost in my mind when I over-rode the opposition to attempting a rescue. I was moved quite simply by the look on the face of the boy who had asked me to try, and who added that the pilot in the sea was his greatest friend.

It was not until we were 3 or 4 miles offshore that we noticed for the first-time splashes from the heavy shells evidently being fired by the battery at Berneval. They caused no damage, and our slow journey back was uneventful as the weather became overcast, and enemy air attacks diminished.

As we approached mid-Channel I asked the Admiralty whether destroyers from the Nore Command could be sent to escort the landing craft to Newhaven, thus allowing the *Calpe* and our own destroyers to increase to their best speed and make for Portsmouth, where 550 wounded soldiers and our own Naval casualties could be landed much sooner and sent to the Royal Naval Hospital at Haslar. The Admiralty's response was immediate, and before night fell, when we were approximately 20 miles south of Newhaven, two destroyers joined me under the command of Captain J.S. Stevens, to shepherd the landing craft into Newhaven.

My own six destroyers then increased speed and reached Portsmouth shortly after midnight. The *Fernie* continued as guide, and *Calpe* took station at the rear of the line because of her damaged steering gear and defective compass. As we approached Portsmouth dockyard, I decided that we ought to invert the line so as to ensure that *Calpe* could take an inner berth without undue confusion. This was desirable in view of the fact that she had as many seriously wounded men to land as all the rest of the destroyers put together. It was a pitch-dark night, and I made the signal with some trepidation as we passed Fort Blockhouse. I thought it possible that none of the young commanding officers had ever performed or even seen this manoeuvre before, yet it was faultlessly executed, and I could not help feeling proud to belong to a service whose young officers could display such professional skill after 24 hours of unremitting exertion and danger.

As we approached the jetty, the dockyard presented an unforgettable sight. It was floodlit, and a veritable sea of ambulances awaited us. They had been assembled by order of Admiral James in his capacity as Deputy Regional Commissioner. They were quickly filled and driven via Fareham to Haslar, while a small army of Police halted all other traffic. Meanwhile, every available doctor in Portsmouth, Havant, and Gosport areas had been told to proceed in advance to the hospital. By their prompt and energetic action, I am sure that Admiral James and his staff were instrumental in saving the lives of many a soldier and sailor.

On arrival alongside I was met by the Admiral himself, and then drove with David Astor (who was serving as a Captain Royal Marines on the C.O.H.Q. public relations staff and had been sent down by Mountbatten), to the Commander-in-Chief's room at Fort Southwick. After telling David Astor and Commodore Duke (Chief of Staff to Admiral James) as much as I could about the raid, we were joined by the Commander-in-Chief, who had with him the two senior Canadian Generals, Sir Andrew McNaughton and Crerar.

Rather to my embarrassment, General McNaughton made a short formal speech conveying a message of thanks from the Canadian Government for the Navy's work in supporting the Canadian division and bringing back so many survivors. Finally, I got to bed at about 03.00 hours, aided by two kind Wrens who got off my shirt, which to my astonishment was caked with blood and firmly stuck to my shoulder and arm.

After an early rise the following morning, David Luce and I drafted a long signal to the Admiralty and Chief of Combined Operations, giving the best preliminary report we could. After attending to urgent business, we then drove to London to be present at a large meeting at C.O.H.Q., presided over by Mountbatten and attended by Brendon Bracken (Minister of Information) and a gallery of Press and Public Relations men. All three Force Commanders were present on the platform and a large number of officers who had taken part in the operation were present in the body of the room. Each Force Commander gave his own account of the raid, after which Mountbatten asked for accounts from any of the officers present.

Leigh-Mallory immediately protested that his own subordinates must report first to him, and he forbade any R.A.F. officer to speak. He added that he felt sure that I would agree. Of course, he was quite right technically, because the Commander of Forces in action has an inalienable responsibility for which he must answer at the Bar of History. It follows that he has a right to insist that all reports by his subordinate Commanders are submitted in the first instance through him. Yet my own position was different insomuch as I still held an appointment on the C.O.H.Q. Staff, while my command of the Naval Forces that had been engaged at Dieppe had lapsed with the conclusion of the operation.

Like Agag, I had to walk delicately. I therefore said that, while I had no objection to any Naval Officers present giving their own accounts, I hoped they would confine themselves to matters of which they had direct knowledge which fell within the sphere of their own responsibility and which was relevant, otherwise they must expect to be interrupted. Despite this warning, one young Lieutenant Commander, who had obviously lunched very well, announced cheerfully that one of the landings had failed because "the troops were yellow". Mountbatten silenced him at once, but the harm was done. The following day I ordered an enquiry, which was carried out by Captain Gibbs, a retired senior captain in command of H.M.S. *Queen Emma*. This enquiry showed that there had indeed been a few isolated instances of troops being reluctant to leave the protection of their landing craft when under heavy machine gun fire – especially when there was no officer on board to lead them. But it was ridiculous to ascribe the failure of any landings to this cause.

In my despatch to Admiral James, I referred to this enquiry, a copy of which I sent separately to him, and which he did not send on to the Admiralty, who did not ask for it. We both felt that no useful purpose would be served by tarnishing the name of a respected regiment, or the memory of men, all of whom had died. Unfortunately, when my despatch was published after the war, the reference to this report was not omitted, and something which had best been allowed to slumber has been referred to in books published long afterwards.

What, it may be asked, did we really learn from Dieppe, and was it worth the price in blood and suffering? Immediately after the raid, Mountbatten set up a Study Group within C.O.H.Q. to examine the operation in detail, and to prepare a report on all the lessons learned. I much admired the speed and energy with which this was done, and the frankness with which the conclusions were given the widest circulation. The first of these conclusions was to stress the need for heavier support, and this was accepted without question. Yet it is in fact an over-simplification. Certainly, there was a need for heavier support, but this had been fully realised by those taking part in the operation even before it took place. As I have already explained, Mountbatten,

Leigh-Mallory and I had pressed in vain for battleships and/or bombers. But what was needed even more was a means of giving the troops effective support after they were ashore – a means of identifying and destroying targets of opportunity, such as concealed machine-guns firing from camouflaged pill boxes. This was not so much a question of weapons as of methods. Although we put in a great deal of time to developing methods during 1943 and 1944, we never really succeeded in solving the problem. When the invasion came, we still had to rely in the main on overwhelming fire support up to the moment of landing.

My own conclusions on the lessons learned were a little different in emphasis, and I can best summarise them by quoting from my official despatch, which was sent to the Commander-in-Chief, Portsmouth on 30 August (ten days after the battle) and published in the *London Gazette* on 12 August 1947.

Here are the relevant quotations:

> Para. 7. 'Although from purely a military point of view the results achieved were disappointing, and heavy casualties sustained regrettable, it is considered that the operation was well worth while provided its lessons are carefully applied when the time comes to re-enter France on a large scale. The principal lesson appears to be, firstly, that much stronger military forces are required to break through the German coastal defences in any important area; secondly that a very much higher proportion of the military force should be held in reserve until the progress made in the initial assaults is known, and that this reserve should then be employed in exploiting success. Unless this is done there is no guarantee that any of the beaches will be properly secured, and this is an absolute pre-requisite of success whether the subsequent phases of the operation are to take the form of a withdrawal or a further follow up.

> 8. A further point that was very clearly shown, is the strength of the German defensive system in the coastal regions, which confronts assaulting troops with the problem not dissimilar to that of the Western Front in the last war. Arising out of this is the need for far more effective methods of supporting the troops, unless it is quite certain that defences which dominate the landing places can be over-run by a surprise night assault. The methods whereby effective support can be given are not considered to include night bombing.

> 9. From the purely Naval point of view the operation has taught us less, if only because the passage and landings went very largely according to plan.

> 11. The operation was interesting also as being perhaps the first occasion on which light naval forces (i.e., coastal craft and landing

craft) manned almost entirely by the Royal Naval Volunteer Reserve, have been employed on a large scale and under conditions of extreme difficulty. They acquitted themselves well, but the small leavening of experienced regular officers of the Royal Navy who were employed in positions of control was an important factor in the results achieved.

12. I consider that the chief lessons of the operation are:

(i) It was shown still to be possible to achieve tactical surprise in a cross-Channel operation of some magnitude.

(ii) The comparatively small naval forces which took part in the operation sufficed to prevent the enemy from offering any surface opposition whatever, apart from that resulting from the chance encounter of Number 5 Group with German armed trawlers.

(iii) If it should be necessary to attempt a frontal attack on strongly defended enemy positions again, it will be essential to provide far more effective means of supporting the troops. In this particular operation I am satisfied that a capital ship could have been operated in the Dieppe area during the first two or three hours of the operation without undue risk.

(iv) The enormous possibilities of this type of operation for bringing about a decisive air battle were demonstrated.

There were other lessons which could not have been appropriately included in a purely naval report, but which I noted inwardly and applied as far as possible the following year when serving as Naval Chief of Staff for the planning of the invasion. Very briefly they include the following:

I. The need for a permanent Assault Force – at least as a nucleus around which big forces could grow.

II. The need to lay down standardised procedures for the conduct of landing craft.

III. When troops are tactically embarked in landing craft, the leading plans should be harmonised as between the Army and Navy; that is to say a recognised unit of Infantry or Armour should be embarked in a recognised unit of the appropriate landing ships or landing craft, and the detailed leading plans should be prepared by the respective Naval and Military Commanding Officers. This idea was anathema to the Army "movements" people even as late as

August 1943, because it conflicted with the idea of getting as much into each landing craft as was theoretically possible.

IV. Dieppe showed that the conventional idea of landing infantry on or before first light in the hope that they could secure a beach through which armour could pass when it grew light, and secure a bridgehead, would have to be re-thought. The same lesson was demonstrated again in the big amphibious assaults in Italy in 1943. It was first publicly discussed at the *Rattle* Conference in June 1943, and completely new tactics were adopted for the Normandy landings in 1944.

V. The Military plan for any large-scale amphibious operation must be sufficiently flexible to allow for reasonable errors in time and place of landing.

VI. The Naval Commanding Officer of big amphibious operations must have his own "Admiral's Wavelength" for the passing of orders to ships and craft – preferably by W/T and preferably in code. The R/T sets installed in every landing craft must be used primarily for broadcasting information and be used with restraint. At Dieppe the volume of R/T traffic was immense and no Naval Commander could possibly assimilate all the signals which were received, let alone take action upon them.

Looking back again to the great battle that was fought off Dieppe, my chief impression at the time, and my outstanding memory after all these years, was its intensity. The din was continuous and unbelievable. This was largely due to the fury of the air battle which began almost as soon as it grew light, and continued without intermission for hours on end. The sky seemed full of parachutes, and whenever one looked up from reading signals, one could see a young man floating down. They included one German pilot, who swam to, the *Calpe,* waited at the back of the bridge for a lull, and then formally declared himself our prisoner. He proved to be a medical student of five or six years standing, and he asked for permission to help the wounded, which was readily granted. During the rest of the day, he won golden opinions from our over-worked doctors.

Did Dieppe lead us to think that invasion was practicable or not? My own reply to that question was that after the raid I was sure that invasion in the central Channel area was practicable, given the right forces, properly trained and armed with the right weapons, and I was sure that I now knew how the assault should be planned. To the best of my knowledge and belief, Leigh-Mallory reached exactly the same conclusion. Certainly, from Dieppe onwards we worked in complete harmony, both in connection with the abortive raids that were mounted under our joint command between August 1942 and May 1943, and also during the outline planning for the invasion, at Norfolk House.

Dieppe has posed some questions that are still unanswered. Immediately after the raid, Leigh-Mallory was of the opinion that the German air losses probably totalled nearly 400 aircraft, certainly there were signs of great confusion on the part of the German Air Command. Towards the conclusions of the raid, we were actually attacked by enemy night training bombers which had been sent from Norway. Leigh-Mallory told me that he felt sure that the German Air Commander would be replaced. But no such thing occurred. But he felt that he must have concealed the extent of the losses from his own superiors and passed them off as cumulative losses during subsequent and preceding operations. After the war German estimates have been accepted which are so low that no-one who was there could believe them.

Another mystery about the raid is why it should have led the German Army Command to think that we should attack the place again when we invaded. People who had visited Dieppe and looked at the remains of tremendous fortifications there have often asked how we could have imagined that the raid would succeed. The answer is that the fortifications were put up afterwards, and not before.

But, of course, the crucial question is whether the operation was justified. In the light of events I myself have no doubt that it was – although I would concede that the same lessons could have been learned more cheaply had we been able to resist the pressure to make a frontal assault. Yet it would be wrong to exaggerate the losses.

Out of 4,963 Canadians who took part in the raid, 907 were killed or died of wounds, and a further 592 were wounded. Over 4,000 survived the battle, though many of them as prisoners of war. This was a grim price to pay, yet it was cheap in comparison with the lessons that were learned, through which the Normandy casualties were enormously reduced.

Chapter 5

"FORCE J"

The weeks that followed the Dieppe raid were a busy period. First, there was my report to be prepared, and I was most anxious to get this completed while the events were still fresh in my mind and before there could be any question of either myself, or anyone else who had taken part, yielding to the temptation to rationalise their actions in the light of subsequent knowledge. It has always struck me as a weakness of so many despatches from generals and admirals that they often take so long to compile. Accordingly, my report was completed and submitted to the Commander-in-Chief, Portsmouth, with copies direct to the Chief of Combined Operations, on 30 August: that is to say ten days after our return to harbour.

To make this possible, I adopted an expedient which afterwards caused some confusion. The core of my report was entitled "The Force Commander's Narrative" and it was a description of the operation as it had appeared to myself and David Luce at the time. While I was at work on this, my staff prepared a longer account which was entitled "A Narrative of Events", which was compiled in consultation with every available source of information from surviving officers in all three Services. Naturally there were inconsistences between the two accounts, but the value of "The Force Commander's Narrative" was that it had at least the merit of making our decisions during the battle easier to understand.

The second urgent task was to submit a list of names for honours and awards. Originally, I had been told by the Admiralty to apply for a total of 50 Decorations and 100 Mentions in Despatches. These figures, I was given to understand, were in accordance with the usual scale that was in force at that time of the war, and it was based on the total number of officers and men who took part in the operation. Subsequently, and before my names had been submitted, I received verbal instructions to double the numbers and apply for 100 decorations and 200 Mentions.

It was not until 29 September 1942, when I had the honour of explaining the whole operation at some length to His Majesty the King, that I learned it was upon the King's personal initiative that the change in numbers had been made. To select so many officers and men for honours is a big and invidious task, and I have been ever grateful to Captain Ryder, V.C., R.N., to whom I delegated the task. He was aided by a small committee of carefully selected officers who had been there, and between them they put an enormous amount of work into their task. The care with which this work was done was shown by the fact that all the recommendations were approved without alteration, and that only two or three young officers wrote subsequently to complain they must have been overlooked.

Meanwhile, by far the most important matter for discussion was the question of whether a permanent Assault Force should be created, made up in the first instance of the surviving ships and craft which had taken part in the raid. This was the proposition which, as already explained, I had put forward just before the raid took place, and it was more controversial than might appear at first sight.

It marked a fundamental change of policy and threatened both the size and the future of the "Combined Operations Command" as it had been established and developed since 1940. It also involved tying up coastal craft and possibly two or three destroyers in a role which was to be primarily concerned with training. It was not surprising, therefore, that those senior officers at C.O.H.Q. who were responsible for administration and training were unenthusiastic; neither did I expect or receive any support from the Operations Divisions of the Admiralty Staff, who were permanently short of ships and men. Mountbatten himself was at first rather guarded in his attitude, since he could hardly come out openly in support of my ideas without giving offence to numbers of much older and devotedly loyal officers on his own staff at C.O.H.Q. However, the matter was handled by the Deputy First Sea Lord, Admiral Kennedy-Purvis, who presided at a meeting at the Admiralty convened a few days after the raid. Knowing that Admiral Sir William James was very much in favour of my proposals, I was dismayed to learn that he did not intend to go to the meeting himself.

On the contrary, he told me that his presence would be unnecessary, and that, for that matter, my own presence would be unnecessary except as a matter of politeness. 'All you need to do', he said, 'is to have nothing to add to your letter, and then remain completely silent. You are in the strong position of having conducted a great amphibious operation, which is more than can be said of any other officer who will be present at the meeting.' Things turned out exactly as the Admiral had forecast, and the meeting lasted less than an hour, and it was decided in principle to recommend the creation of the permanent force.

To begin with it compromised the ships and craft which had taken part in the Dieppe raid, and it was christened "Force J" because the Dieppe raid had been known as Operation *Jubilee*. Despite the obvious reservations at C.O.H.Q. about this development, once the decision was made, "Force J" had no more staunch or friendly supporter than Mountbatten himself, and, thanks to his example, it developed and grew with consistent and friendly unfailing help from the C.O.H.Q. Staff as a whole. Thanks also to the goodwill of Mountbatten and the Second Sea Lord at the Admiralty, the staff I had been given for the raid continued with me in my new appointment as Senior Officer "Force J".

Although the prime role of "Force J" was to train and expand so as to be ready for the invasion of France when it came, there was a natural tendency in its early days to focus attention on further cross-Channel raids. Leigh-Mallory for example, was tremendously in favour of a large-scale feint operation in which no troops should actually be landed, the landing craft turning back when within 2 or 3 miles of the shore, but which should present a sufficient threat to some part of the enemy coastline to bring on another great air battle. Together we planned an operation on these lines, which was given the code-name *Aflame*. It never took place, largely on account of persistent bad weather, but we all stood by to carry it out from 3 to 10 October. Meanwhile at C.O.H.Q., their operational staff had evolved a plan for a large airborne attack on the Island of Ushant.

This operation was called *Crucible* and was intended to take place before the end of September 1942. It involved dropping practically all the airborne troops that were available, but even so their numbers were judged insufficient to ensure the capture of the western part of the island where the only decent harbour is situated. Accordingly, they were to be taken off by the Assault Ships, who were to anchor in the Baie de Stiff, which is situated on the eastern side of Ushant in the narrow sea passage between Ushant and the mainland. The Baie de Stiff is more or less semi-circular, with a radius of only 1 cable (200 yards), or 400 yards across the entrance. Unfortunately, there are rocks bang in the centre of this entrance, and at Spring Tides the tidal stream across the entrance runs up to 11 knots.

At first, I took a somewhat passive interest in this plan, until I was asked to attend a meeting to discuss the operation on 16 September. This meeting, which was presided over by Mountbatten, eventually approved the operation, and it was then that I discovered for the first time that I was cast in the role of the Naval Force Commander!

What concerned me most were the navigational hazards of taking a couple of ships of some 5,000 tons each into this tiny bay with less than 200 yards in which to pull up after passing the rocks at the entrance at what would have to be a high-speed owing to the tremendous cross currents.

I remember writing privately to the hydrographer of the Navy to ask his opinion on what the conditions would be like. In his reply he summarised them in a single phrase – "Awe Inspiring" – and added that at least my name would go down to history in one of those footnotes to the Admiralty Sailing Directions which would probably read: 'It was here in 1942 that H.M.S. *Prince Charles* and her consort, H.M.S. *Prince Albert* were cast away and became total wrecks.' Nevertheless, the planning went forward, and on the night of 25 September I proceeded to Plymouth with the two Assault Ships and four Destroyers.

On arrival I met the Air Commander, who on this particular occasion, and on this occasion only, was not Leigh-Mallory, but the Air Vice Marshal commanding that Group of Coastal Command, which worked alongside the Commander in Chief, Plymouth – Admiral of the Fleet, Sir Charles Forbes. I found on arrival that Sir Charles had even greater misgivings than myself, but he added hopefully 'perhaps the weather will be kind'. In contrast the Air Vice Marshal struck me as not being fully seized of the hazards of this operation, for which he had been temporarily allocated two squadrons of Leigh-Mallory's Spitfire IX.

On 27 September, which was a Sunday, the weather conditions struck me as being quite favourable, but those with local knowledge maintained that there was a considerable risk of meeting a heavy Atlantic swell on the other side of the Channel long before one got as far south as Ushant. Accordingly, I went out in a motor gunboat and we proceeded at full speed to a position about 75 miles south-west of Plymouth, to see whether there were any signs of an increasing swell.

On the contrary we found the conditions absolutely perfect, and I returned to Plymouth with the intention of sailing for *Crucible* that same evening. On arrival I found that the operation had been cancelled. I never discovered the exact reason, but I do know that the Spitfire IX had suffered heavy losses during a preliminary operation to bomb the two big German airfields near Brest. Later the same week I found that Leigh-Mallory was still too angry to discuss the matter, as he had lost some of his most brilliant pilots.

During all this period I was much preoccupied in trying to find a suitable headquarters from which to run "Force J" and which would not involve sharing Fort Southwick with the Commander in Chief, Portsmouth's large staff. The Admiralty were anxious that I should make use of the large and elaborate headquarters that had been established at Osborne Court on the sea front of East Cowes.

At the time the pros and cons of using these headquarters at Cowes seemed to be evenly balanced. There were obvious advantages in moving into a place which was already elaborately fitted out, with sufficient self-contained blocks of offices to supply the needs of even the largest staff, and which also had the necessary equipment to make it a first-class communications centre, including a whole floor fitted out to meet the needs of a large cypher staff.

Again, it was obvious that for some time to come the whole of "Force J" could be berthed in the Portsmouth/Southampton area, and the upper stories of Osbourne Court gave a commanding view over almost the entire Solent, including, of course, the approaches and entrance to the River Medina. Furthermore, one half of the flats were still available for use as accommodation, and therefore offered an ideal site for housing the large body of W.R.N.S. (running into several hundreds) which I was advised would be required by the administrative side of my staff. Finally, there was the attraction of going to an area which had already been commissioned as a naval establishment under the name of H.M.S. *Vectis*.

Vectis was well supplied with boats and had a small "Ship's Company" to keep the area clean and do the chores. On the other hand, it was not clear where I myself, my personal staff, and the key Staff Officers could live in Cowes, on top of which I felt reluctant to be cut off from the mainland by the Solent because I realised that there would be many meetings at C.O.H.Q. which I should have to attend. However, the Solent did not seem so great an obstacle, even in thick fog or during the winter gales, provided some of the navigational M.L.s which were to be attached to "Force J" could be berthed in the River Medina.

My personal accommodation problem was solved in a most luxurious way through the kindness of the Royal Yacht Squadron's Committee. They offered to let me have the Royal Yacht Squadron Castle at a peppercorn rent of 1/- a year, provided I agreed not to disturb the existing furniture, or to make use of their famous wine cellar without the agreement of one or two members of the committee. In addition, they asked that their old Wine Butler, Frederick, should be allowed to continue to carry out his duties in the cellar, and also that their secretary – a retired Paymaster Captain – should be allowed to continue to use the tiny office he had in the Castle.

The Castle can accommodate sixteen people in comfort in addition to the domestic staff with which I was supplied. I therefore decided that in addition to the Chief of Staff, my secretary, and my Flag Lieutenant, those Staff Officers who were necessarily privy to all the secrets should live in the Castle and mess with me. This made eight of us all told, and left ample room to accommodate visiting Generals, Air Marshals, and similar V.I.P.s.

I am bound to add that Lord Mottistone (who was the moving spirit on the Squadron Committee in all these arrangements) was not actuated by altruism, as he frankly stated at the time. They were all terrified that the Castle would be requisitioned by the Army and used to accommodate robust young soldiers who might not have the same respect of those hallowed precincts as a group of senior naval officers.

All these arrangements were quickly made, and we moved over to the Isle of Wight and occupied our new headquarters and the Squadron Castle, on 12 October 1942. As time passed and "Force J" steadily grew in size, so also did the space that we needed. From the beginning we had had the Marine Hotel, which was used to house the Ship's Company. The Officers were at first accommodated in the Island Sailing Club which had been requisitioned. Later on, we took the adjacent Gloucester Hotel and another Yacht Club building. The growing force of beach signalmen occupied a Butlin Holiday Camp in Gurnard Bay, while the large "Castle Rock" Victorian house immediately inland of the Castle was used as the Brigade Headquarters of one brigade of the Royal Marine Division (which from the beginning was under my operational command, and whose troops were accommodated on the island).

For journeys to London or elsewhere on the mainland, I always landed at a pier at Warsash, which gave access to a Naval Establishment called H.M.S. *Tormentor*, which was under my operational command and accommodated all our L.C.P. It was here, incidentally, that my official car was kept.

Other "Force J" bases in the area included the Old Docks at Southampton, where five assault ships were berthed, and also two or three flotillas of tank landing craft. We also kept one flotilla of tank landing craft on the Beaulieu River, while David Beatty, who commanded the whole squadron, used Exbury House as his headquarters. As "Force J" grew, we began to overflow from the Solent group of bases and were obliged to establish increasing numbers of landing ships and craft at Portsmouth itself, and Newhaven, and later on at Weymouth.

Life at Cowes was extremely busy, but also very pleasant. Although I had innumerable visitors, chiefly in the form of Generals from Home Forces, but also including Mountbatten himself who came twice for a night or two, one enjoyed a remarkable degree of privacy in the Isle of Wight, and I must confess I found it agreeable to be the "Monarch of all I surveyed".

Only twice was our privacy disturbed. In the spring of 1943, a German fighter/bomber made a tip-and-run attack on the Castle. Its bomb burst on the famous Squadron Lawn, creating an unsightly crater.

I myself was away at the time, and Sir Godfrey Baring (the senior member of the Royal Yacht Squadron Committee and a very good friend to me) wrote to tell me about this act of desecration, and remarked 'These devils stop at nothing'. However, a greater threat came from a visiting Admiralty Official, who informed us that our occupation of the Squadron Castle as tenants paying a peppercorn rent was grossly improper. What upset him most was the fact that the stair carpet had not been taken up. According to the regulations by which his life was ordered, only Commanders-in-Chief were allowed stair carpets. He said that the building would be requisitioned at once; all the furniture would be put in store; and "utility furniture" of an approved design and on an approved scale would be purchased and installed.

I asked Admiral St. Leger Moore, who by this time was serving in the rank of Captain as Head of the Administrative side of my staff and as Maintenance Captain, to hold this jealous little man in conversation for as long as he could. Meanwhile, I rang up Henry Markham (Secretary of the Admiralty) and told him of the threat with which we were faced. I have seldom heard anyone laugh so heartily, and we heard no more about the matter.

Indeed, life at Cowes was not without its lighter moments. Every morning before breakfast it was my practice to take an early morning run as far as Egypt Point and back. When Brigadier Reading, who commanded the Royal Marine Brigade which was based on the island, heard about this, he decided that his young soldiers ought to go for a run as well. The first I knew of this was when I found myself surrounded by a great throng of runners as I approached Egypt Point.

It was very dark and impossible to see who they were. Fortunately, they could not see who I was – because I found I myself was the sole topic of conversation and learned in lurid terms exactly what they felt should be done to me. But worse followed: when I reached my point of turn at Egypt Point, a ferocious Sergeant told me to carry on with the rest, with the result that I had to run an extra 2 miles as I felt that this was no moment to disclose my identity. However, as the morning grew lighter, most of the Marines had apparently developed a taste for an early morning run, and when I was recognised, I found them more than friendly and talkative.

On Saturdays and Sundays, I took a long cycle ride or went to the local cinema, depending on the weather. David Luce had discovered that a Sub-Lieutenant Sexton, R.N.V.R. to whom we had given command of one of the new L.C.S. (S), after he had performed an act of great gallantry in rescuing the crew of a very small support craft which capsized off Rye, was himself an ardent cyclist, and he had arranged for Sexton's craft to be berthed in the Medina and for his cycle to be housed next to mine in the Castle's precinct. I suspect that David's object was to keep me occupied and quiet over the weekend.

It certainly did so, because young Sexton did not consider we had started our ride until about 40 miles had been covered. He looked about 18, but must have been a bit more since I discovered he was married with five children. He was nevertheless a most charming companion, and by talking to him every weekend I got to know what the younger officers were thinking about our activities. Most tragically, Sexton was killed while his craft was playing a decisive part in the storming of the Island of Walcheren.

It was while I was at Cowes that I first noticed the extraordinary change in the attitude of the younger generation towards my generation. It became increasingly noticeable that the young conscripts of 1943 had far better manners than earlier generations of their age, and were equally losing their sense of a "generation gap", but liked to make friendly conversation on appropriate occasions with senior officers. I remember going to see a film one Saturday afternoon, just after I had been made a Commodore First-Class and was therefore dressed up as a Rear Admiral.

The cinema was very empty, and I sat down in the middle of a completely empty row. Two or three rows behind there were a couple of young Beach Signalmen – the equivalent of Ordinary Seamen – during the interval they both rose to their feet, not in order to leave the cinema as I had quite expected, but to move into my row and sit next to me and make polite conversation. Such a thing would have been impossible in the pre-war Navy, where the average young sailor would have moved a long way to avoid being too close to a Flag Officer.

Another rather amusing interlude in our lives occurred shortly after the murder of Admiral Darlan. Winston apparently thought that this might be the start of an "Assassination Campaign" directed against key Commanders. I was flattered to find myself included in this category, and supplied with a motor cycling guard of rather ferocious young soldiers. One of them was always posted at the entrance to the Squadron Castle, while another stood at the entrance 100 yards away to the offices in Osborne Court. Whenever I drove to London, I was obliged to have two of these heavily armed and decorative protectors as outriders ahead of the car, while a third followed behind. The ones in front were trained to keep a fixed distance from us, and whenever we increased speed, so did the two motor cyclists. I regret to say that we never solved the problem of what to do if our guardians took a wrong turning, which happened from time to time.

During the three weeks that these young men were with us they made a mass conquest of all the W.R.N.S., and one of my older and more staid Staff Officers had an embarrassing experience in consequence. As I mentioned earlier, part of Osborne Court was used to accommodate our W.R.N.S., who used the same entrance as the staff. On this occasion, the girlfriend of one of the soldiers had entered the building to retrieve something she had left behind, while the soldier waited outside. Almost immediately afterwards the Staff Officer left the building to go out and have dinner. It was an exceptionally dark night, and the rather elderly officer was surprised at finding himself seized in a passionate embrace because the waiting soldier assumed it was his girlfriend returning to him!

Reverting to more serious matters, Operation *Aflame* had no sooner been abandoned and dismounted than the planners at C.O.H.Q. proposed a new operation which had the code-name of *Clawhammer*. This operation was directed against a radar station of somewhat limited importance at the tip of the Cherbourg Peninsula. The troops designated to carry it out comprised almost the whole of the Special Service Brigade available in the United Kingdom; that is to say between 7 and 8 complete Commandos. The Military Force Commander was Bob Laycock (who afterwards became Chief of Combined Operations, and later Governor of Malta at a difficult time), while Leigh-Mallory and I were once again the Air and Naval Force Commanders. *Clawhammer* was first thought of early in October and was intended to take place during November – a somewhat unlikely month to find the necessary forecastable period of fine weather.

There were three or four other operations on the table, though after this lapse of time I forget their names and their objectives. But throughout September and October we stood by night after night to carry out whichever operation appeared most suited to the prevailing weather and tidal conditions. In addition to this, I was instructed to make an attempt to intercept a large German supply ship bound for one of the Atlantic U-boat bases which had got as far as Dunkirk.

For this purpose, I was given seven or eight Hunt-class destroyers, together with all the steam gunboats. Numerous attempts had been made, and were yet to be made, to try to cut the German coastal route to the Atlantic ports because it was thought that the French railway system was unable to cope with the supplies needed by the U-boats at the zenith of their offensive. However, we never succeeded in closing the route, and one reason, so I was told, was that experience had shown that it was not advisable to operate both destroyers and coastal craft in close mutual tactical support. The Commander-in-Chief, Portsmouth was unwilling to accept this limitation, and he asked me to carry out a sweep along the enemy coast on the night of 11/12 October, based on carefully co-ordinated operational plans.

Accordingly, I put to sea in H.M.S. *Fernie* on that night followed by the destroyers. Meanwhile, the steam gunboats sailed from Newhaven with orders to close the French coast and sweep to the westward, rendezvousing with my Destroyer Force somewhere off Dieppe. I soon learned why operations which depended on tactical co-operation between coastal craft and destroyers were difficult. The night was dark and the sea rather rough. The destroyer station-keeping under those conditions left much to be desired, and my force of eight ships must have extended for over three miles from van to rear.

On arrival at the rendezvous there was no sign of the steam gunboats, so we swept slowly westwards as the dawn came. In due course the light improved sufficiently to see Dieppe for the second time in two months, and it looked very much the same as it had looked in August. At this moment some small craft could be made out approaching from the direction of the harbour and the Captain of the *Fernie* said that he felt sure they were E-boats. David Luce and I felt equally sure that they were the steam gunboats about 20 miles out of position. But at this moment our rear destroyer in the line made signal for "enemy in sight" and opened fire. Furthermore, we could get no reply to our challenge.

Accordingly, we increased to full speed and led the destroyers back towards Dieppe, opening fire at the same time. Despite an impressive volume of fire for about five minutes, no hits were obtained. And then, just as I was beginning to wonder whether it was advisable to approach the enemy coast any closer, one of the E-boats made the correct coded reply to our challenge, and we realised that they were the steam gunboats after all.

It was now time to return to Portsmouth, which was accomplished without incident. Nothing was seen at any time of the German supply ship, and we learned subsequently that she had been turned back to Dunkirk.

Living with several different raiding operations mounted simultaneously, and standing by to carry one of them out, night after night, was rather a strain. Indeed, on one occasion we found just after we had sailed that my secretary had got mixed up and brought the wrong Operation Orders with him. Fortunately, the Captain of the ship in which I was embarked had been issued with a spare copy.

Once I was installed in the Isle of Wight, I had a hard think and concluded that if training was to be our main object, we must have a "closed season" for raids during the winter – if only because the time and effort they involved was out of all proportion to the prospect of being able to carry any of them out. Leigh-Mallory felt the same, although for some differing reasons. He told me that he had strongly opposed *Clawhammer* in particular because he felt no confidence that the troops would establish a firmly held beach-head, and that it would be a case of Dieppe all over again.

At his suggestion, we both wrote identical letters expressing our unwillingness to carry the operation out. The letters were addressed personally to Mountbatten, with copies to the First Sea Lord and the Chief of Air Staff, respectively. These letters received instant approval from the Chiefs of Staff and the operation was cancelled within 48 hours of their being despatched. At last, I had time to think about the future of "Force J", which had in the meanwhile been seriously depleted of its landing craft by the needs of the North African campaign.

The first tasks were three-fold: to standardise signals; to produce standard Fighting Instructions; and to establish a bombardment range at which it would be safe to fire at targets of opportunity under most weather conditions.

Let me say a word about each.

For generations the Naval Signal Book have given special meanings to Signal Flags when hoisted singly (e.g., No.5 Flag means "Open Fire"; another numeral Flag means "I am in danger of sinking from enemy gunfire", and another means "Chase", and so forth). In more recent years certain Flags or Burgees could be used singly as orders to the ships in Company to make an emergency turn. It was not until after the Dieppe Raid was over, and we got down to regular exercises at sea with a mixture of ordinary R.N. ships, landing craft, and coastal craft that I discovered that the training ships at Combined Operations Headquarters, and also at Coastal Craft Bases, had endowed many of these single Flags with different meanings more appropriate to the special work which landing craft and coastal craft were likely to be engaged upon.

Although this was a good idea in theory, it could be distinctly awkward when the different types of ships and craft were operating in company. On one occasion when I was at sea with a composite force of destroyers, tank landing craft and motor gunboats, we were closing the Needles Rocks from the south and at the same time carrying out a bombardment of some targets which had been painted on the face of the perpendicular cliffs at the western end of the Isle of Wight. The visibility was patchy and uncertain, but I was very anxious to complete the bombardment exercise and then return to harbour. Just as it was ending the fog suddenly began to thicken, so I hoisted a signal which ordered an emergency turn to port, since we were getting close to shoal water.

When it was executed, the destroyers all turned together as I had expected, but the tank landing craft began to lose headway and disappeared from sight in the fog. Meanwhile, the gunboats apparently went mad and disappeared at high speed, steering apparently in every direction. Eventually we all got back to harbour and at the ensuing post-mortem I discovered that the signal meant "Stop engines" to landing craft, whereas, made to coastal craft, it indicated "Take up stations to repel an imminent attack by E-boats"! After this I insisted that all units in "Force J" must be prepared to accept the meanings given in the official signal books, and I am afraid this decision caused a certain amount of heartache among the veteran members of the Combined Operations Training Establishment.

The establishment of a "Bombardment Range" presented no difficulty at all. There was a sparsely inhabited piece of land running from about a mile to the east of the Needles Rocks to about 5 miles to the east: that is to say its eastern boundary was a little to the west of Totland. There were in all only nineteen cottages and small houses in this area, and each could be clearly marked on a special chart/map which we had printed. I had on my staff a Major Gibb, who served as "Army Liaison Officer". He suggested that if we only used the range twice a week between, say, 9 in the morning and 5 in the afternoon, it would be easy for him to round up all the inhabitants of these houses and cottages and have them driven (rather like so many refugees) to the Hotel at Yarmouth, where they could spend the day.

Punctually, at 17.00 hours he would collect them and return them to their homes. They were paid a generous subsistence allowance for their day in the hotel and compensation was promised in the event of any damage being done to their property. This arrangement, strangely enough, was extremely popular with the residents, despite the fact that before long we were using the range four days every week.

After all, the alternative was to requisition the whole bit of land and have it wired off for the duration of the war, in which case all the people in the area would have to find alternative occupations. Indeed, I believe the "Force J" Range was quite unique so far as the way we ran it was concerned. General Paget professed himself to be green with envy, and told me that throughout the U.K. he always had the utmost difficulty in establishing a range on which his troops could fire live ammunition. From time to time, I must admit that we had some narrow squeaks. On one occasion a destroyer carrying out a bombardment exercise from the seaward side of the range, fired a very wild 4" shell, which burst in the garden of a small cottage at the extreme south-eastern end of the range.

Major Gibb was appalled, because the cottage in question was occupied by a 95-year-old naval pensioner, who had persuaded the Major to allow him to remain in his cottage that day, since the official target area was at the other end of the range at least 3 miles away. The Major dashed over in his Jeep to see what had befallen the old man, and arrived while the whole garden was still enshrouded in a cloud of dust. On entering, he saw the pensioner, still sitting in a chair in the garden, covered with the feathers of some unfortunate chickens which had been even closer to the point where the shell burst, but when he urged the old man to get into his car immediately, the reply came, 'Let me be. Let me be. I likes a bit of gunfire.'

Major Gibb was a remarkably practical man, who had become a stockbroker when he retired from the Army some years earlier. I eventually discovered that the true secret of the popularity of the range and of its acceptance by the local people lay in Major Gibb's extremely practical way of paying compensation. When he returned the people to their houses, he always carried a pouch crammed with bank notes. Whenever there appeared to be signs of damage to a property, he would ask the owner how much damage he wished to claim. Then, in nine cases out of ten he would say that this was much too low an estimate, and that in his opinion nothing short of £10 was reasonable, and the £10 was paid there and then. Although this may seem extravagant, and would not, I am quite sure, have been approved by the Treasury, or by the Admiralty Officials, it none the less must have saved an enormous amount of money in comparison to what formal requisitioning would have cost the country.

The short task of producing some standard "Fighting Instructions" proved the easiest of all. We drafted what were called the "Force J

Fighting Instructions" (short title "F.J.I.s") simply by going through a typical raid chronologically, starting with the assembly of the ships and craft, continuing with their passage to their objectives, followed by a chapter on the assault, ending with one on the withdrawal. In which case it was easy in the light of the Dieppe Raid to lay down standard methods which would be followed unless otherwise ordered. Shortly after this work had been completed, and the instructions promulgated, I was visited by an American Admiral, whose name now escapes me, but who was currently charged with the training of the rapidly growing American fleet of landing craft and assault ships.

The Admiral was most appreciative and complimentary. He wrote afterwards to say that the "F.J.I.s" were being adopted more and more by the U.S.N., particularly in their far eastern operations against Japan. Before the end of 1943, we re-wrote the "F.J.I.s" under a more general form which we thought would be appropriate for a large-scale invasion, as opposed to a raid. Chapters were added to deal with the follow-up, and build-up, after the initial assault, while the chapter on withdrawal was greatly curtailed. In their new form the instructions were entitled "General Instructions for the Conduct of Naval Assault Forces" (short title "G.I.C.N.A.F."). These instructions were adopted by Admiral Ramsey when he was appointed Naval Commander-in-Chief for *Overlord* and remained in force until the end of the war.

The Squadron Castle proved a veritable magnet which drew a wide variety of distinguished personages to call on me. Agreeable though this was, in many ways it also proved extremely expensive, because even if the Admiralty had re-imbursed one for each visit, life was too short to handle the paperwork that would have been involved. On 24 October 1942, for example, a signal from the Admiralty reached me after breakfast to say that General de Gaulle, who was coming to visit the Free French Naval Base at Cowes, wished to come after that to the Castle for luncheon, and for a private discussion of a personal nature. We rang the Free French base, where the French Chasseurs were berthed and had their being, and learned that he would arrive at the Castle at precisely noon, and would be accompanied by ten or eleven Staff Officers. It was rather short notice to arrange a suitable luncheon on that scale; however, my large retinue of W.R.E.N. cooks and stewards worked wonders, and by inviting Lord Mottestone and Sir Godfrey Baring to join the party, I gained access to the squadron's cellar!

I had little doubt about the nature of the private business which de Gaulle had in mind, because his son – then Midshipman de Gaulle – was serving in a fast Vedette attached to the Cowes base, and the speed at which he liked to roar up and down the Solent had already attracted a good deal of comment. Meanwhile, we were pestered with rather unhelpful advice from the Admiralty: could I strengthen the local air defences during the period of the General's visit? I consulted Leigh-Mallory on the direct line which connected our respective headquarters, and he recommended anchoring a couple of flak craft in the mouth of the Medina, just off the Castle, and this was done.

I then asked the Admiralty whether the General should be received with a Guard of Honour appropriate to a Head of State, or to a General. To which the reply came 'You should use your own discretion'. In the end we decided to land the A.A. Guns crews of one of the two flack craft. The men concerned were regular Marines and still had their peacetime blue uniforms. They numbered approximately eighty all told. In the end the size of the Guard was regulated by the amount of space between the entrance gate to the Squadron precincts and the entrance door of the Castle itself. The result was a Guard much larger than a General would have received, but somewhat smaller than what was laid down for a Head of State. However, de Gaulle was visibly delighted, and inspected the ranks of the Royal Marines in a slow and majestic way. At that time, he had no English in the ordinary sense, but at the end of his inspection he addresses the officers in command of the Guard in a loud and clear voice: 'Thank you very much for allowing me to inspect your beautiful soldiers.' It says much for the discipline of the Royal Marines that not a man smiled.

After a short and friendly discussion about his son, during which I was careful to disclaim all responsibility, we went into lunch. I found that despite my poor French I could understand every word that de Gaulle spoke, largely, I think, because he spoke so slowly and expresses himself in such simple language.

I was particularly struck by his eyes, which conveyed an impression of deep tragedy, much as he must, no doubt, have felt within him.

When the fish course came, some rather special French wine was served, and the General's eyes suddenly filled with tears. He apologised and explained that the wine brought back so many memories to him.

Before lunch was over, he told me that the day was a sad day for the French Navy, because he had just initialled an agreement which would permit the old battleships *Paris* and *Courbet* to be broken up for scrap metal. These ships, which had been built in 1912, were hardly of great naval significance, but required a large number of sailors to look after them. I immediately asked the General why he had not given them to me for use by "Force J". 'Why', he then asked, 'Do you not demand the *Victory*?' I explained that the '*Victory* was made of wood', while the old battleships were made of steel, and heavily protected with armour plate.

David Luce who was sitting the other side of the General, strongly backed me up, and explained that the old and well protected ships which could be treated as expendable were often in demand for a combined operation. We reminded him of the *Vindictive* at Zeebrugge, and more recently of *St. Nazaire*. 'But when, Monsieur', he pressed me, 'do you foresee the *Paris* and the *Courbet* being used?' 'On the day of the liberation of France', I replied, rather vaguely, but grandly. Suddenly the General's manner changed, and holding out his hand to grasp mine he said 'Monsieur, they are yours'.

Shortly afterwards he left with many expressions of cordiality and mutual respect. I regret to add that after his return to London there was a very considerable row. The Foreign Office were upset at receiving a letter from de Gaulle explaining that for the first time since he had come over to England, he had been received with a Guard of Honour appropriate to his position, and would they confirm that this was a precedent. He then informed the Admiralty that his agreement to the scrapping of the battleships was revoked, and he had given them to me. The Controller of the Navy at that time was the late Admiral Wake Walker, and I have seldom spoken to an angrier man on the telephone. It had apparently taken him six months to persuade the General to agree to the scrapping, and now all was in the melting pot again. The Admirals parting shot to me was, 'Two battleships exchanged over the luncheon table - whoever heard of such a thing?!' But de Gaulle kept his word.

Curiously enough, the two ships did play a part in the liberation of France, but not quite in a way which either the General or I myself had foreseen. They were used as the centre-piece of the great barrier of sunken ships off Arromanches which gave shelter and protection to the artificial harbour, and when I went there in 1954, their fighting tops were still visible.

General de Gaulle was a strange man. Not one word of thanks did we receive for the entertainment and luncheon which we had provided, but many years later (in 1960, when I was a member of the Western European Union Assembly and Rapporteur for the Control and Inspection of Arms under the 1954 Paris Agreement), he sent me a message by Monsieur Liquard who led the French delegation, to say what happy memories he still had of his visit to the Isle of Wight.

The variegated activities took place against a background of almost continuous exercises. Most of these were limited in size and were conducted within the Solent area or in Poole Bay. In some cases, troops from the Royal Marine Division, from the Guards' Armoured Division, and from Nos. 40 and 41 Royal Marine Commandos, were embarked and practiced in assault techniques, but some exercises were purely Naval. H.M.S. *Locust* proved to be an admirable Headquarters Ship so long as no Army Commanding Officer and his staff needed to be embarked. She had accommodation for six of my staff, and also for Third Officer W.R.N.S. Miss Towle, my faithful and efficient stenographer.

On average I spent two or three days a week embarked on *Locust* and while so embarked, the administration of "Force J" and its bases was delegated to St. Leger-Moore. Early in the life of "Force J", however, I became concerned at the extent to which the landing craft were dependent on the support of their bases. This was understandable, and perhaps inevitable, in the case of the small, or "minor" landing craft, to give them their official designation. It was wholly unnecessary, and quite unacceptable so far as major landing craft were concerned. For example, there was no uniform system for feeding the tank landing craft crews when they were away from their base.

They were in the habit of going ashore for their meals and even when away from their base, no victuals were supplied from Naval sources; instead, every officer and man was placed permanently on "Subsistence Allowance" and left to fend for himself. In consequence, the standard of messing, which depended on the housekeeping experience of the officers and men concerned, could be very high, and could equally well be deplorable. Meanwhile the pay of all concerned was approximately double because the subsistence allowance was generous, and also tax free. Similarly, the maintenance of major landing craft was over dependent on the Flotilla and Squadron Maintenance Staff, who usually lived ashore at the base.

I therefore decided to see what would happen if I took "Force J" to Portland and spent the month of January there. Portland is no distance by sea from the Solent (about 70 miles) and possesses one of the finest artificial harbours in the world. It is, however, notorious for its winter gales. The Admiralty could not have been more astounded at this decision had I proposed to go to Vladivostok. Every obstacle was placed in my way. 'The Force would be destroyed by aerial bombing', I was told. 'It would be impossible to provide at Portland sufficient coal to fuel the coal-burning assault ships: The harbour would be too exposed, and not large enough for my small Force' and so on, and so forth.

I naturally consulted Leigh-Mallory, who at about this time had succeeded Sir Sholto Douglas as Commander-in-Chief. Fighter Command. He agreed that "Force J" might well prove an attractive target for the Luftwaffe, but he was confident that he could provide the necessary protection. Accordingly, a number of Squadrons were moved from the south-eastern area into Dorsetshire, and an impressive number of multiple Bofors guns were mounted at intervals all along Chesil Beach, which connects Portland with the mainland.

In addition, the Admiralty Stores Department established a considerable stock of coal on the quayside of the small dockyard at Portland. There was a complication inasmuch as one assault ship could only burn "Midland Washed Knobs", while the *Invicta* consumed "Kentish Washed Knobs (small)". During our stay the supply of these special fuels became very short, since I had not realised that if these vessels had to lie at anchor with steam raised for safety reasons, they ran out of fuel within 24 hours! We experimented to see whether the two different types of Washed Knobs were inter-changeable, and established that they were not.

Eventually, I moved in *Locust* to Portland on 7 January 1943, taking with me four assault ships, twenty-four tank landing craft, six flotillas of raiding craft (seventy-two craft in all) and a number of coastal craft for escort and navigational duties. We arrived without incident on the same afternoon, and I immediately called on the Flag Officer-in-Charge, the late Sir Carlisle Swabey, who was distinctly nervous at this invasion of his territory, although most friendly and co-operative.

The first unforeseen difficulty which we discovered as soon as we secured at the "Flag Ship Buoy" was that the telephone equipment at Portland ran on a different voltage to the rest of the country, with the result that the special cypher machine installed in the *Locust* would not operate. The obvious solution would have been to transfer some of our cypher staff at Cowes to Portland, but Admiral Swabey was against this as he felt it would be regarded as a slight upon his own cypher staff. It was not long before the team at Portland changed their minds when they discovered the volume of encyphered messages which reach us every day from the Admiralty.

Whenever the weather permitted, we took the whole Force to sea for exercises, and before long the landing craft became quite proficient entering and leaving harbour in company, and accurately to a timetable. Nevertheless, we had our fair share of gales, and there were times when I felt sure that we should lose some of the tank landing craft on the somewhat rocky breakwater. Yet we survived, and the only casualties were two raiding craft which sank at their moorings through bumping together in the Scend caused by an unusually strong gale.

It was during the stay at Portland that "Force J" was supplied with a small sample of a new type of "minor" landing craft, especially designed for landing troops on rocky beaches. They were constructed on the same lines as a Whitby Cobble and I regret to say that we tested them to destruction during the very first exercises in which they took part.

During the first ten days or so of our stay at Portland, the morale of the crews of both the landing craft and the coastal craft fell to a low ebb, but afterwards their spirits rose rapidly as they discovered that they could, after all, be self-supporting and self-maintaining.

I returned on 27 January to Cowes, with the whole Force in good shape and good heart, having accomplished exactly what we set out to accomplish; namely to prove that even minor landing craft could safely be operated for two or three weeks on end while far away from their bases and relying on themselves. This was clearly a matter of paramount importance, since no invasion of France could hope to succeed unless the landing craft which would carry the troops on "D-Day" could look after themselves during the weeks that might be needed to establish a secure beachhead.

At about this time Admiral Sir Charles Little succeeded Sir William James as Commander-in-Chief, Portsmouth. At the end of the war, he began his report on Operation *Overlord* by remarking that it was the successful visit to Portland, and survival of "Force J" in the month of January 1943, that had first convinced him that the invasion of France was a feasible operation.

I must now digress to say a word about the activities of the Small-Scale Raiding Force during the winter of 1942 to 1943.

Not long after my arrival at Cowes, March-Phillips called and told me that since his small but successful raid two days before Dieppe, he had achieved nothing, and he was convinced that the naval authorities were prejudiced against him so long as he was independent. He may have been right, and I could not help feeling a little sympathy with the officers who served on the staffs of the Commander-in-Chief, Portsmouth, and the Commander-in-Chief, Plymouth. After all, they were up to their eyes with administrative work, and such operational duties as they had were primarily concerned with the protection and smooth running of coastal convoys which were routed through our own coastal waters.

Only rarely did vessels under their orders operate in enemy waters, apart, of course, from coastal craft. Moreover, it was about this time that Admiral James was succeeded by Sir Charles Little as Commander-in-Chief, Portsmouth. Admiral Little was a senior admiral with a long record of operational work. He was a man of high intellectual calibre and a stickler for going about things in the correct, orthodox way unless there were strong reasons to the contrary. I feel sure that he felt no such reasons existed for the small-scale raiding force "set-up" which, in fact, led to small operations, which were basically naval, to being directed by a young, and not too articulate, Army officer. Be this as it may, the object of March-Phillips's visit was to swallow his pride and ask whether I would take the S.S.R.F. under my operational control, and if so, would I give him my word that my staff would not obstruct, so long as were happy about the Naval aspect of the raids, which he contemplated. I readily gave this undertaking, and had no difficulty in securing the agreement of Mountbatten as Chief of Combined Operations, and of Admiral Little, who was my immediate local supervisor. Indeed, Mountbatten lost no time in regularizing the matter by the issue of a revised Directive which made me the Operational Authority for the Small-Scale Raiding Force, subject to two reservations:

(i) All raids must be based on suggestions and Intelligence from C.O.H.Q.

(ii) The maximum number of troops to be landed was not to exceed 200 without special authorisation.

A few small raids, each involving at most eight soldiers, were quickly and successfully carried out. In most cases the troops and their Goatley boat were carried in a non-operational motor torpedo boat and were escorted by one or two craft from the 14th Motor Gunboat Flotilla. This flotilla was permanently attached to "Force J" and was commanded by Lieutenant Commander Nye, D.S.C., R.N.V.R., an officer of considerable experience in whom I had complete confidence. Each of his craft was fitted with special navigational aids, and by employing them as escorts to the Small-Scale Raiders, we killed two birds with one stone. This was because Nye's motor gunboats were at the time engaged in a survey to check the accuracy of "QH" at various points all along the French Coast from Boulogne to Brest.

One of the earlier small raids took place during the visit of "Force J" to Portland. The raiding craft sailed from Dartmouth, and the orders laid it down that the final signal ordering the raid to take place would be made not later than 22.00 hours on the night when the raiders had to sail. Accordingly, David Luce and I studied the weather carefully before going to bed, and felt satisfied that conditions would be perfect, as indeed they were.

The following morning, I was told that a success signal had been received during the night, and that the raiders, who had suffered no losses, were expected back at Dartmouth almost at once. We had scarcely made a congratulatory signal when Peter Howes arrived rather shaken, and showed me a signal from the Admiralty calling for an immediate signalled report, followed by a full written report on why I had carried out the operation notwithstanding the prohibition contained in an Admiralty message, whose number was quoted. The immediate reply was quite simple: namely that the Admiralty message had not been received.

Within five minutes the *Locust*'s Officer of the Watch reported that the Flag Officer-in-Charge was approaching in his barge, and I went on deck to receive Admiral Swabey, who arrived, very flustered, at about 08.30 hours. He explained that owing to mistaken zeal on the part of his senior W.R.N.'s Cypher Officer, a signal which should have been sent off to me the night before had been kept to show him first, when he got up in the morning. This was the missing Admiralty message!

The W.R.N. officer's reasons were, firstly, that it had arrived at midnight, and she thought it rather too late to disturb Admiral Swabey; secondly, that as it merely said that something should not take place, she felt it could not be urgently important, and thirdly, that it bore the prefix "Hush-Rush". She had never seen these prefixes on a signal before and felt, therefore, that once again her own Admiral should see it first. Actually, the prefix "Hush" meant the highest degree of secrecy – even more secret than "Top Secret", while "Rush" meant the highest degree of urgency, even more urgent than "Most Immediate".

I am afraid I merely made a further signal to the Admiralty saying that the report they had called for would be furnished by the Flag Officer-in-Charge at Portland.

We never discovered the reasons why the Admiralty had wished to cancel the operation, and since it was extremely successful, I could not help feeling glad that the mistake over its cancellation had been made.

Very soon after this, David Luce informed me that he was having some difficulty with March-Phillips, who, he thought, would wish to see me to state a complaint. His complaint was that my Chief of Staff would not agree to a small operation, involving March-Phillips himself, an N.C.O., and two "other ranks" on which he, March-Phillips, had set his heart. The operation was in the form of a raid on a very minor objective extremely close to Le Havre and it only differed from other Small-Scale Raids inasmuch as the four raiders were to spend 24 hours hidden in a cave in neighbouring cliffs, and fetched off during the night after they had landed.

David Luce flatly refused to agree that this raid should be carried out. He could not see what purpose commensurate with the risks would be served, and he had a deep premonition that it would result in the death or capture of March-Phillips and his companions. Equally, I could see that this particular raid had become an obsession with March-Phillips, although he never disclosed to me, or so far as I know to anyone else, his true purpose in wishing to hide in the cliffs for 24 hours before he attacked.

That he had some purpose I had little doubt, but to this day I have never been clear what it was. What was quite clear, however, was that March-Phillips would never be satisfied until he had his way. In view of my promise to him that I would not obstruct his plans except on Naval grounds, and in view of his unbroken record of success in this type of small raid, I eventually agreed that it should go forward. David Luce said that my decision was tantamount to agreeing that the raiders should be allowed to commit suicide. In the event he was proved right.

After the death of March-Phillips, the command of the Small-Scale Raiding Force devolved on Captain (as he was then) Appleyard. Appleyard was an entirely different type of man to March-Phillips. Aged at that time about 25, he was very clear and precise in his speech: Like March-Phillips he was totally devoid of fear: but he approached every operation with ice-cold, ruthless, efficiency. If Appleyard said a particular plan was sound, one could be certain that it was sound, and that he would carry it out whatever might befall.

During the winter and early spring months of 1942 and 1943, we mounted no less than fifty small-scale raids, and carried out thirty-seven. The great majority of these were under Appleyard's command, and with rare exceptions they all went exactly as planned. The cumulative effect of the small-scale raids was hard to evaluate, but from such Intelligence reports as reached me it seemed that it was not inconsiderable, especially along the coast of Brittany. The Germans had been in the habit of watching the coast by means of small cycle patrols of, perhaps a corporal plus four other ranks.

These patrols were a favourite target of the raids, which made the German troops progressively more nervous. Even before the winter was over there was evidence that the patrols had been drastically strengthened, thus tying down substantially more troops on what was an essentially static and defensive role. Yet the raiders were not unwelcome to some young German soldiers.

One raid was carried out on the lighthouse on the Casquet Rocks with the object of putting the lighthouse out of action and bringing the French keeper and his wife and family back to England. According to our information there was no one else there, but to the surprise and amusement of the small-scale raiders it was found that there was a "garrison" of six or eight young soldiers. They were surprised in bed, asleep in pairs, with their hair beautifully arranged in hair nets. There was no resistance, and the young men made little attempt to conceal their relief at being out of the war.

The biggest small-scale raid was on the Isle of Sark, and involved, I think, over 100 troops. The garrison was believed to amount to one Company, accommodated and stationed at one end of the island. The plan was to land at the other end of the island and to advance rapidly and noisily towards the position of the German Company. About half the raiders were to halt half way along the island and remain in ambush. The plan worked well, save for one unforeseen event. A German fortification expert of high rank was visiting Sark on the night of the raid, and he was accompanied by between 100 and 200 pioneer type troops, presumably to carry out his directions for strengthening the fortifications. These wretched men were no match for the raiding troops. Indeed, they were not fighting troops at all. They were accommodated in the camp near the beach where our men landed.

Confronted by what I suppose were fighting men as formidable as any in Europe, they instantly surrendered to a man. Appleyard did not hesitate: leaving a Sergeant and three or four other ranks to keep an eye on the prisoners, he pressed on with his plans and inflicted heavy losses on the German garrison. As the time passed, the prisoners began to realise how few their guardian were, and they became restive. A few actually tried to escape, and the Sergeant tried to have them tied up to prevent this. Yet some succeeded in making off and were shot.

The tying up of prisoners is specifically forbidden by the Geneva Convention, and, after the Dieppe raid, the German High Command had made a great fuss because the Canadian Operation Orders, of which a copy had been captured, contained advice that if prisoners caused trouble in landing craft they should be tied up. So, when this actually happened on Sark, Herr Hitler screamed the house down, and all the prisoners taken at Dieppe were tied up as a reprisal for about a year. Oddly enough, Herr Hitler said little or nothing about the German troops who were shot while escaping: that was something he understood perfectly.

Before the summer of 1943 was over, I was visited by a Brigadier from the War Office who had come to inspect the Small-Scale Raiding Force. He told me that their administration was not up to War Office standards, and that there would have to be a complete re-organisation. Meanwhile, they must stop operating for a few weeks. Although he did not say so, he inferred that he was to supersede Appleyard. David Luce and I agreed that we had seen the last of the Small-Scale Raids, and I was not surprised when Appleyard told me a few days later that he was applying for a new job. He joined the Airborne Troops and went to his death in a Mediterranean Operation only a few months later. His passing was a grievous loss, but at least he had lived long enough to write a small but glorious page of Military History.

The manner in which the Small-Scale Raiding Force faded out left a nasty taste in my mouth, and was not a typical of the times. Nothing was more dangerous than for a young officer to win success and fame. More senior officers could be relied upon to muscle in and supersede them. When I reported to Admiral Little on these events, I remember how he said nothing for a time, then murmured, half to himself: 'The pot-hunters -the bloody pot-hunters', which he repeated over and over again. Within six months he himself was destined to fall victim to "Pot-hunters" operating on a much greater scale.

Early in 1943, the famous Casablanca Conference took place at which it was decided to defer the invasion of France until 1944, and to give priority to Mediterranean operations throughout 1943. At first it seemed that that this must mean the end of "Force J". However, the decision curiously enough had the opposite effect. Mountbatten decided that all the additional landing craft which were now coming forward should join "Force J" as soon as they had been commissioned and completed their work-up trials. While in "Force J" they should be formed into squadrons and flotillas, as appropriate, and given their operational training before being sent out to the Mediterranean as formed units. In consequence the average size of "Force J" rapidly grew, and judging from the letters which I received from Naval Authorities in the Mediterranean, they were well satisfied with the arrangement.

It was, however, decided that by the end of the Combined Operations season in the Mediterranean, "Force J" should be allowed to grow and be stabilised at the size required to lift one complete division. After this, new assault forces should be formed to lift each additional division designated for the assault when France was invaded.

To match my growing responsibilities, I was made a Commodore First-Class, and hoisted my broad pennant at the Royal Yacht Squadron Flag Staff on 30 March 1943. This rare distinction gave me great inward elation. Commodores First-Class are uncommon, and "in commission" (that is to say in command, as opposed to being on a staff) they are very rare indeed. When they are made, they are usually senior Captains due for promotion to the Flag List before their job is likely to end. But I had less than three years seniority as a Captain. The advantages of this translation were numerous.

Apart from doubling my pay, it entitled me to a very much higher grade of Secretary and Secretariat, and also to a Flag Captain to handle the administrative side of our work. This was immense, and before the year ended, "Force J" numbered no less than 15,000 officers and men and comprised 28 assault ships, some 200 tank landing craft, about 40 Landing Craft Infantry (Small), a large number of the American-built large Landing Craft (Infantry). Two or three flotillas of motor gunboats, all the steam gunboats, about 18 motor launches, and a similar number of Landing Craft (Flak) together with a considerable force of assorted types of support craft.

Another decision of the Casablanca Conference was that the outline plan for the invasion of France should be made during the latter half of 1943, before any officers had been appointed in command of the operation. The idea was that this work should be carried out in London in offices established at Norfolk House, St. James's Square. The officers responsible for this important piece of planning should work under the chairmanship of a Lieutenant General holding the appointment of Chief of Staff to the Supreme Allied Command (Designate). Lieutenant General Sir Frederick Morgan filled this appointment (short title "COSSAC") and proved to be a first-class Chairman. Then there were to be two officers of Rear Admiral's or equivalent rank, one being called Chief of Staff to the Naval Commander (Designate) and the other Chief of Staff to the Allied Air Commander (Designate).

The officer appointed on the naval side as Naval Commander-in-Chief (Designate) was Admiral Sir Charles Little, with Vice Admiral Sir Philip Vian as his Chief of Staff at Norfolk House, with the title of C.O.S. (X).

Meanwhile, I received instructions to plan and prepare for the capture of the Channel Islands. The Air Commander was to be Leigh-Mallory, by then Commander-in-Chief, Fighter Command, but no one was specifically named as Army Commander, although the Forces that could be used were known and comprised the Guard's Armoured Division, the Royal Marine Division, all the Commandos available in the United Kingdom and also the airborne troops available in the U.K. The intention was to carry out the initial assault in the month of July to synchronise with the invasion of Sicily. The operation was given the code-name *Constellation*, and we were given astonishing latitude to decide the sequence in which the islands should be attacked. A separate code-name was allotted to each, and all began with the syllable "Con". Alderney, which Leigh-Mallory and I agreed should be tackled first, was called Operation *Concertina*.

No great amount of work was involved in the planning of *Concertina* since we were able to make use of the detailed plan that had been prepared for the abortive attack on Alderney in May 1942. There was, however, one major difference. We now had twelve L.C.I. (L), each capable of carrying 300 troops, which gave a lift for 3,600 Infantry, which was well in excess of the number which it was proposed to land in the assault. The superior speed of these craft (12 knots as against 5 or 6 knots in the case of L.C.A.) was a very great asset, and as we only needed eight for the assault it was possible to obtain a qualified Navigating Officer for each one.

"Force J" by this time also possessed no less than eighteen L.C.F., each of which carried 8 Pom-Poms or twin Bofors anti-aircraft guns. Leigh-Mallory had great faith in the efficiency of the L.C.F. as a means of deterring attacks by low flying fighter bombers, which was the form of attack which he found it most difficult to counter with his fighters. On this occasion we planned the heavy saturation bombing which was to proceed the landing with more detail than had been done the year before. It was to take place in three phases with a ten-minute interval between each phase. We thought that this would deter the island's garrison from leaving the shelter of their bomb-proof dug-outs too soon after the bombing had ceased. We also enlisted the help of the famous "Pathfinder" Squadrons by laying lines of coloured flares to mark the ends of each of the landing beaches.

On the whole, both Leigh-Mallory and I felt far happier about this modified plan for attacking Alderney than we had about the original plan. Perhaps I should add that it was intended, as far as possible, to use nothing but experienced Commandos for the first assault.

Early in April I sent the L.C.I. (L) together with H.M.S. *Locust* and a number of L.C.P. round Land's End to Milford Haven, and I proceeded there myself by air a few days later. The idea was that the Milford Haven area, with its strong tidal streams and numerous small beaches with rocks at either end of them, would prove a good place from which to practice the L.C.I.(L) in entering and beaching themselves under conditions not dissimilar from those to be found in the Channel Islands.

On my arrival, however, I acted on local advice and moved on to Fishguard. On the short passage there we routed the L.C.I. (L) and indeed the *Locust* as well, inside, and indeed in between the Bishop Rock. It was evident that the lighthouse keeper thought we were quite mad, and through my binoculars I could see him frantically waving a red flag. Nevertheless, it was a good opening exercise for the somewhat inexperienced R.N.V.R. captains of the L.C.I.(L) to see what was involved in keeping station while passing through narrow channels with cross tides of anything up to 8 knots.

By 15 April, I was satisfied that the L.C.I.(L) could be relied upon to carry out the task that would face them at Alderney, and, after a final briefing meeting, I returned to Cowes. On arrival I was confronted by a signal from the Commander-in-Chief, Mediterranean (Lord Cunningham), which was addressed to the Admiralty, supporting a request from Admiral Ramsay that all the L.C.F. should be transferred to his command and take part in the invasion of Sicily. The request, I soon learned, was strongly opposed by Mountbatten on the grounds that we already had overwhelming air superiority in the Central Mediterranean, and that it was highly unlikely that the L.C.F. would reach Sicily in time to take much part in the operation. However, notwithstanding his representations, and notwithstanding the fact that Admiral Pound had some reluctance in withdrawing the L.C.F. from Operation *Constellation*, Admiral Ramsay's request was approved. Leigh-Mallory at once rang me up, and said that in his judgement we should both write similar letters declining to proceed with our operation.

I was most reluctant to take this course as I had always believed, and still believe, that the capture of the Channel Islands, followed by the capture of the Cherbourg Peninsula itself, would be a most valuable prelude to the main invasion. It would have greatly reduced the hazards of that operation by extending to the Brittany Peninsula the area in which a major landing operation would have been possible, and thus greatly lengthening the coastline which the Germans would have to be prepared to defend.

However, Leigh-Mallory pointed out that if we lost the L.C.F. the precedent would have been set, and it would not have been long before the Mediterranean command made further demands at the expense of "Force J". The Air Chief Marshal took what I thought at the time a most cynical view of what was going on. He described it as a game of "Beggar-my-Neighbour" in which you pinch the forces of your professional rivals in order that they would be unable to operate, and all the operations would fall into your lot. In the light of what happened later in the year I believe that there was indeed something to be said for his theory.

However, as events turned out, I had little time for speculation because Admiral Mack, who had been designated as one of the Naval Force Commanders in the Mediterranean operations, was killed in an air accident. Admiral Pound felt that the only Admiral with the necessary experience to take his place at such short notice was Sir Philip Vian: accordingly, Sir Philip's appointment as Chief of Staff (X), was terminated almost before it begun, and I was appointed in his place. It was further decided by the First Sea Lord that I should only continue as C.O.S.(X) until the outline plan for the invasion had been accepted and approved by the Prime Minister and President, after which I was to return to "Force J", which would be the chief of the assault forces taking part.

Accordingly, I moved to London on 7 May and worked at Norfolk House until 16 August. During my absence, David Luce exercised what was described as day-to-day command of "Force J" but continued to refer policy decisions to me, while I went to Cowes for week-ends whenever I could get away from London.

Between the time that I returned from Fishguard and the time I moved to London, I spent about a week at sea in the *Locust*, during which time I visited a number of small landing craft bases on the south coast between Poole and Ramsgate. These bases did not come under "Force J", neither at that time did the landing craft which used them. These craft were mostly minor landing craft, and totalled about 1,000. They were craft intended for the "build-up" phase of the invasion, and were not required for the initial assault and "follow-up". They were mostly kept out of the water, and their crews, which were only then beginning to arrive, lived ashore. Naturally, their efficiency depended largely on the personality of the Officer-in-Charge of the Base.

For some time, my staff had been most concerned about these officers, some of whom were advanced in years, and of very varied energy and activity. They all came under a very retired senior officer in the C.-in-C. Portsmouth's staff, who was believed by my own staff to be much too easy going. However, I had no direct evidence of the shortcomings of the bases. That is why I decided to visit them while I still had time, and while it was not too late to substitute younger and more energetic officers for what would soon become very responsible work.

I took with me in the *Locust* David Luce, my secretary (Lieutenant Commander Kitson), and the Force Navigating Officer, without whose help I doubted whether the *Locust* would succeed in entering some of the smaller places. The trip was not without its amusing moments, and achieved its object inasmuch as a majority of the base commanders were replaced almost immediately. Nevertheless, it inevitably led to a certain amount of unpleasantness, but I have always been glad that we got this over before I left for London.

The making of the outline plan for Operation *Overlord* is a story in itself, which I shall summarise in the next chapter.

Chapter 6

PLANNING FOR *OVERLORD*

On 27 April 1943, while still at Cowes, I had a long talk with Sir Philip Vian and urged that now might be the time to release David Luce and myself for general service and appoint someone to command "Force J" who would be likely to stay in that appointment until the invasion had been carried out. "Force J" at the moment was small, and it would take some weeks, if not months, to build it up again under the guidance of its new commander, whoever that might be. Three days later, Admiral Little sent for me to say that Sir Philip's appointment as C.O.S.(X) was cancelled, and that I was to replace him pro tem, leaving David Luce to exercise day-to-day command while I was in London.

On 1 May, I drove to London and attended my first "Staff Meeting" at Norfolk House, with General Morgan in the Chair. Planning for *Overlord*, I found, had scarce begun. But there was already a nucleus of a Naval Staff, the senior officer of which was Commander Cresswell.

I formed the opinion that Commander Cresswell and his subordinates were dejected and bored, as well they might be. They had been at Norfolk House ever since planning for the North African campaign had started. With the departure of General Eisenhower and Admiral Ramsay to execute those plans, they were given a general directive to bring the plans for the invasion up-to-date. Although there were a number of Army and R.A.F. Staff Officers at Norfolk House engaged on the same task, there was no officer with the authority, or indeed the knowledge and experience, to make even a provisional decision on where the landings should be made, or how they should be followed up.

Any plan they could make could therefore be no more than a "Staff Study" of a highly theoretical nature. It was hardly surprising, therefore, that they had become rather cynical and had ceased to believe in the reality of their work. For several days after 1 May, I travelled each morning to London and returned by car and motor launch each evening in time for dinner, followed by paperwork connected with "Force J". Much of my time while in London was spent at the Admiralty lobbying for a stronger staff. In the end I obtained two first class commanders to serve as Staff Officer (Operations) and Staff Officer (Plans). In addition, Captain Robert Mansergh (now Admiral Sir Robert Mansergh K.C.B.) was appointed as Deputy Chief of Staff. Bob Mansergh was a lot senior to me on the Captain's List and was an officer of the highest calibre and integrity.

I was deeply grateful to him for condescending to work under me, and he brought to our work as a whole, an attention to detail which was foreign to my nature, and which was much needed. As my secretary I was able to retain Commander Kitson, while Captain Brian Edgerton (Ret'd.) agreed to serve as Assistant Chief of Staff, with a special responsibility for logistics, as we had now learned to call them.

Brian Edgerton had been my Captain in 1933 when I was a Lieutenant Commander in H.M.S. *Courageous*. He was a man of brilliant intellect and great charm. He was also talented in other ways, notably as a landscape painter. Unfortunately, his hearing was beginning to fail, and this greatly distressed him when taking the Chair at meetings, because he had such difficulty in following the trend in the discussions.

During this same period, I was taken by Admiral Little to have luncheon with Admiral Stark, U.S.N., who was the Senior Naval Representative of the United States in London. Admiral Stark was a firm friend of the British, and a man of considerable kindness. He strongly agreed with my wish that the Naval part of the staff at Norfolk House should be fully integrated as between American and British Officers, and Commander Elliot Strauss was nominated by him to serve as an Assistant Chief of Staff (U.S.). Sometime later, a Captain Hutchings, U.S.N., was appointed as an additional Deputy Chief of Staff (U.S.). He brought with him a personal note to me from Admiral Ernest King in Washington. Admiral King explained in his note that Captain Hutchings had a record of distinguished operational service in the American Heavy Cruiser, U.S.S. *Augusta* and he made it clear that Captain Hutchings enjoyed his complete confidence. If, therefore, any matter arose which I felt demanded Admiral King's personal attention, he would be grateful if I would inform him through this channel.

I got through one other important piece of business during the opening days of May. My chief anxiety about our work as a whole lay in the fear that we should fail to produce an agreed plan – even in outline – just as the "Combined Commanders" and the "Sledgehammer" Combined Staff had failed during 1942.

In the case of General Morgan's organisation at Norfolk House, the position was in some ways more complex, if only because the three Services were not represented in the same way. For example, the large Army staff at General Morgan's disposal included no-one with executive command over any forces at all. There was a Major General with his own staff for operational planning (Major General West), there was another for logistic planning (Major General Brownjohn), another for intelligence (Major General Whitlock), and so forth.

In addition, there were two senior brigadiers representing the Director of Movements at the War Office. But the actual Forces designated to carry out the invasion consisted of the Second Army and the First Army, and was known as the 21st Army Group. They were under the Command of General Paget, who at that time was also the Commander-in-Chief, Home Forces. General Paget and his staff did not have offices at Norfolk House, but had a separate headquarters of their own. The same was true of the American Army, whose Commander was General Devers, while Major General Ray Barker, U.S. Army, was a member of General Morgan's staff.

In the opposite extreme, the Commander-in-Chief of the Air Forces in north-western Europe had already been appointed; namely Leigh-Mallory, and he, together with some of his senior Staff Officers, had office accommodation in Norfolk House, and did their own planning so far as the Air Forces were concerned. It is true that there was an Air Vice Marshal at first, holding a similar appointment to my own, but Leigh-Mallory soon made it clear that he would attend to planning matters himself. In the case of the Navy, the position lay somewhere between that of the Army and the R.A.F.

Although no Naval Commander-in-Chief had actually been appointed, it was understood that Admiral Little should stand in for him until an outline plan had been agreed and approved, and, because I commanded "Force J", it meant that in addition to being the head of the Naval Staff at Norfolk House, I also controlled the great bulk of the landing craft which at the time were available for the operation.

What, it may be asked, was the position of the Chief of Combined Operations and C.O.H.Q. in this rather complicated organisation? Officially, we were required to seek the advice of C.O.H.Q. on all technical problems connected with Amphibious Warfare. So long as Mountbatten continued as Chief of Combined Operations, C.O.H.Q.'s role was a good deal wider than that. Because of his great reputation and influence, it was obvious that no plan was likely to gain approval of Mr Churchill or the Chiefs of Staff Committee unless it also enjoyed the support of Mountbatten.

Accordingly, a good deal of "Coffee-housing" went on between General Morgan and the senior officers at C.O.H.Q., while I feel certain that the same was true in the case of the junior Staff Officers. But at the intermediate level, such as my own or Major Brownjohn's, we tried to avoid discussion with the C.O.H.Q. Staff until we had at least reached a point at which we were ready with firm proposals. This was partly for reasons of security, and partly because as the responsibility for the outline plan was vested in the Norfolk House Staff, it seemed more proper that we should reach our own conclusions before seeking external advice.

It was partly for these reasons that before doing anything else at Norfolk House, I spent an entire afternoon in the early days of May with Leigh-Mallory at his headquarters at Uxbridge. I found he shared my anxiety lest the dispute between those who favoured a landing in the Pas-de-Calais, and those who preferred the Central Channel area would break out again. But he felt confident that this could be avoided if we both worked closely together and pursued the same tactics. His own views were every bit as strongly in favour of the Central Channel as my own, and, if it came to that, as we believed Mountbatten's views to be. However, Leigh-Mallory was strongly of the opinion that we should both refrain from expressing any opinion on this matter until Major General West and his own Staff Officers had submitted a "Full Appreciation" on the subject.

By this stage the actual directive to which General Morgan had to work had been received, and it was worded approximately as follows: 'To prepare the best possible outline plan for securing a lodgement area in north-west France during 1944 from which a major offensive could be mounted and launched against the German Army in 1945.'

Leigh-Mallory's suggestion was that he and I should refuse to express any opinion on where to land in France until the Army had made up their minds what this "lodgement area" was to be. He maintained that when faced with the problem of where they wanted to get to, the soldiers would themselves be drawn to abandon any idea that they should start from the Pas-de-Calais. Meanwhile, on the assumption that it would take the Generals from two to three weeks to prepare their Appreciation, Leigh-Mallory thought that the R.A.F. and the Navy could best spend the time deciding on the "Chain of Command" during the invasion, as this presented many difficulties to both Services. We followed this plan and things worked out very much as we had hoped.

It was not until 7 May that I left finally for London. Before leaving, I chose one of the numerous young officers who served at the Raiding

Craft Base at Warsash to accompany me to act as my "Personal Assistant" during the time I was at Norfolk House. His name was Richard Fenning, and he continued as my Flag Lieutenant after I returned to "Force J"; he subsequently became Flag Lieutenant to Admiral Power when he was Commander-in-Chief in the Middle East. Richard Fenning was undergoing training in the hotel business at the time of his call up, and he was therefore able to help me in the perennially troublesome task of finding comfortable accommodation for myself at a moment's notice.

Fortunately, I still had a lien on my flat in Whitehall Court, and was able to establish myself there until 20 May, after which, taking advantage of Captain Harrison-Wallace's good offices, we moved to a suite in the Ritz Hotel. In addition to my own bedroom, which overlooked Green Park, and its very spacious bathroom, there was a smaller bedroom for Mr Fenning, another for my Naval valet, and a most well-furnished and sizeable sitting room. Nothing could have been more convenient and comfortable, as it only took a few minutes to walk to Norfolk House, and I had most of my meals in the sitting room.

It was, however, expensive, and it was a financial relief to move in the middle of June to a beautifully furnished house, No.33 Eaton Terrace, which belonged to a friend of mine who had recently been called up and was serving as an ordinary seaman in the Navy. The house at Eaton Terrace I shared with Captain Egerton and Mr Fenning, with whose aid I was able to engage a first class cook, Mrs Woods by name, who had been working as the "Chef" at Flemings Hotel.

The Army Appreciation in what should constitute the "Lodgement Area" was ready for presentation by General West at a plenary meeting held at Norfolk House before the end of May. The General recommended that the Lodgement Area should be in Normandy and Brittany and run from Le Havre to Avranches inclusive. As soon as the General had summarised his recommendations, Leigh-Mallory and I both intervened to say that we agreed in principle, and further that we felt that the landings should be concentrated on the Normandy beaches in the general area between Caen and Beauvais; that is to say in the Baie-de-Seine.

Although the beach gradients were somewhat less than I should have liked, there were no dangerous rocks or reefs offshore, and the whole area was sheltered from the Atlantic swell. The landing craft which we had been told would be available would suffice for two British and one American division to be embarked for the actual assault, plus one British and one American division for the follow-up, during the afternoon of D-Day.

We were agreed that, for an operation of this magnitude, we should need five days of forecastable fair weather – that is to say five days of settled fair weather which could be predicted, say, three days ahead of the fair-weather period. Research showed that, since accurate records had been kept, such weather conditions always occurred once in May or June, and sometimes in both months. Although they were somewhat more common in June than in May, there had been quite a number of years in which June passed without any settled weather. This being so, we decided to make it a condition of our outline plan that all must be ready to launch the invasion from 1 May 1944 onwards.

Before dispersing at the end of the meeting, we agreed to adjourn for a week while the Combined Staffs made a more detailed study for the landings and for their exploitation up to the time when Cherbourg would be captured. This plenary meeting was, perhaps, the most vital that was held during the preparation of the outline plan. As I walked back to the Ritz after it was over, I could hardly believe that the great controversy which had raged for over a year about where to land in France had been settled to the complete satisfaction of all three Services within a month of the start of serious work. However, when we met a week later, we found that all was still far from well. General West and his staff were adamant that it would take three weeks from D-Day before Cherbourg was captured. Leigh-Mallory and I were both deeply concerned of the prospect of having to maintain, what would by then be quite a large Army, over the beaches for so long a time.

It was therefore agreed to adjourn once again for a week while the Army Staffs examined a possible alternative, namely to assault with five divisions instead of three, the two additional divisions being landed on the eastern side of the Cherbourg Peninsula with the object of cutting it off from France and thus expediting the fall of Cherbourg itself. This alternative was discussed at length at our next meeting, which must have been held a few days before mid-June. General West informed us that while he could not rule it out, he nonetheless could not recommend it. It had several disadvantages:

(i) It meant it would involve postponing D-Day until early June, to give time for the additional landing craft that would be required if two more divisions were to be embarked for the assault, to be completed.

(ii) By having only three divisions ashore in Normandy on D-Day instead of five, there was a risk that Caen itself would not fall on D-Day, and that its airfield and its canal system, both of which were vital objectives so far as the R.A.F. and the Navy were concerned, might not be captured for several days.

(iii) Moreover, the General doubted whether, even if the Cherbourg Peninsula was isolated, the Seaport would be captured any more quickly. He felt that the final assault upon it would have to await the arrival of re-enforcements who would have to be drawn from troops landed originally on the Normandy beaches.

Leigh-Mallory and I both acquiesced in General West's conclusions and were ready to accept the plan in its original form. However, General Morgan, who was strangely reluctant to commit himself to anything in the least definite, decided that the final decision on this particular issue should be left to the Supreme Commander when he was appointed, and that meanwhile, our outline plan should merely record the alternatives and set forth the pros and cons of each. As a matter of history, we know from Field Marshal Montgomery's memoirs that he preferred the five divisional assault. In the event, all General West's fears were realised, and Cherbourg still took three weeks to capture.

On 15 and 16 June there was a pleasant interlude while we visited Instow and Barnstaple to witness a large-scale demonstration of a new "Waterproofing" system which had been developed in America for reducing the risk of engine stalling when vehicles disembarked in fairly deep water. This had been a constant trouble ever since large-scale amphibious operations had begun to be practised; the problem was partly a psychological one because experience showed that when the sea water was cold, even the most resolute drivers tended to ease their foot off the accelerator at the moment when the sea reached their crutch! Needless to say, it only takes one stalled engine when a tank or other vehicle reaches the bottom of the ramp to cause a disproportionate delay before those behind it can continue landing.

So great was the importance attached by the American Army to this problem that they were determined to demonstrate their new invention to all and sundry. As always, the demonstration was laid on in a grand and luxurious way.

On the evening of 15 June, we boarded a special train which belonged to General Lee, United States Army, and which was waiting for us in the disused station at Addison Road. Each sleeping compartment was large and luxurious by British standards and was equipped with a "Scrambler" telephone, which was plugged in to the shore telephone system whenever the train stopped. The morning of 16 June found us at Instow, parked on a disused length of railway line which ran through some small sand dunes. We spent the day watching various demonstrations and trials, and holding a number of impromptu meetings. The train started on its return journey shortly after midnight, and I was back in the Ritz at 08.15 hours on 17 June.

Meanwhile, General West's staff had been hard at work on the plan for Military Operations that would follow the fall of Cherbourg. I was deeply concerned to find that they could offer no hope for the capture of Le Havre before three months had elapsed, by which time the Anglo-American Armies might number over 1 million men. Although Cherbourg has a reasonable capacity when one is thinking in terms of one or two Army Corps, it would be wholly inadequate to support an offensive by an entire Army Group. Both Leigh-Mallory and I viewed with profound apprehension the prospect of having to maintain a huge Army for months on end over open beaches, in particular I had an uneasy feeling that the surface of the beaches themselves would deteriorate after heavy tank landing ships and large coasters had been beached on them day after day for weeks on end.

This was something on which we had no experience, neither was there any possible method by which we could obtain the experience before the time came. I racked my brain, trying to evolve some form of gigantic concrete pier which could be floated over to Normandy and sunk opposite convenient beach exits, and at which large ships could berth. However, the technical difficulties seemed insurmountable. The Director of Transportation at the War Office said I must meet Colonel Bruce White (now Sir Bruce White), who had designed what is called a "Spud Pontoon" pier, which would solve all these problems.

I learned that this pier, which had originated in Mountbatten's fertile mind during 1942, enjoyed the active support of Mr Churchill himself, and that a full scale one had been constructed and erected in the Solway Firth. Would I be prepared to go and see it? Rather ungraciously, I said I had better things to do because the Solway Firth has comparatively sheltered water and would afford no indication on how the pier would withstand a northerly gale on the Normandy beaches. However, I did visit the War Office cinema, and saw a film of the pier taken during a strong gale. The usual photographic tricks had been played to make you think you were watching huge seas break against the pier, and certainly there was a very strong wind blowing, nevertheless I was wholly unconvinced.

As time went on none, of those concerned, including myself, seemed to get any nearer in our search for a solution to the problem. Accordingly, after great soul searching, I sent a brief note to General Morgan, on Friday, 18 June, to the effect that unless some method could be found to avoid reliance on maintenance over the beaches for so long a period, I could not continue to support the outline plan in the form in which it was being developed. Leigh-Mallory, with whom I had been in close consultation, sent an identical Minute to the General at the same time.

General Morgan was understandably upset, and told us that he felt we had torpedoed the whole operation. At any rate, he agreed that our respective notes should be the first item on the agenda for a plenary staff meeting to be held on Tuesday, 22 June.

On Sunday, 20 June, I went with Brian Egerton and Richard Fenning, as was our custom, to attend the morning service at the Abbey, and throughout most of the service I turned the whole matter over and over again in my mind. During the singing of the Anthem, it suddenly came to me in a flash that we must, and could, create an artificial area of sheltered water on a Napoleonic scale by sinking a host of block-ships so as to create vast breakwaters within perhaps 12 hours of the original landing.

As soon as the service was over, I left my companions and walked quickly to Norfolk House, where by good fortune the Navigating Officer on my staff, Lieutenant Commander Steel, happened to be on duty as "Duty Staff Officer". I told him of my scheme, and asked him to prepare a plan for the artificial harbour at the most convenient point in the landing area which had already been selected, and I added that I would like to see it as son as I came in on Monday morning. Steel was most discouraging, and thought I had forgotten that the rise and fall of the tide in the Baie-de-Seine is some 25 feet, with the result that only the largest vessels would constitute an effective breakwater at high tide. I told him to study the chart, because I felt sure that there would be shoal water offshore, constituting a natural foundation for any artificial breakwater.

I recollected that during the Abyssinian Crisis in 1935, when we seriously considered creating a Naval Harbour and base at Famagusta in Cyprus, we had found just the same thing. But Steel was not to be mollified so easily. He said that he felt reasonably sure that no such shoal water would be found, and he would get the charts to show me there and then. I told him to study the charts after he had had luncheon, and meanwhile I went to have my own, followed by a visit to the cinema.

On the Monday morning I was greeted at the office by a rather chastened Steel, who had already prepared a beautiful plan for artificial breakwaters off Arromanches. However, he added that, as a matter of interest, he had studied the charts of the French coast all the way from the Belgian border to the Spanish border, and that Arromanches was

107

the only place at which an artificial harbour, such as I had visualised, could be established.

Since Arromanches was right in the middle of our chosen landing area, and since the idea had come to me while attending a service at the Abbey, I felt sure that the Hand of God was with us, and that the harbour would succeed. At our meeting the following day, I told General Morgan that I wished to withdraw my Minute, because it would be possible for us to take our port with us, and I pointed out that the surprisingly slender scale of German defences in the Normandy area could be explained by the fact that they, too, must realise how long it would take an invader to capture the port of Le Havre, and consequently had probably assumed that the Normandy area was a technical impossibility so far as invasion was concerned. In other words, although we could not hope for strategical or tactical surprise, we might substitute technical surprise.

It is worthy to record that unlike most novel projects, there was at no time any obstruction to the artificial harbour project. It needed up to 100 ocean-going ships in its original form, and Bob Mansergh went with some trepidation to broach the matter to Lord Leathers, then Minister of Shipping. He returned with a message from the Minister to the effect that even if we wanted 200 ships, we could have them for such a project. Indeed, from beginning to end the whole idea went forward with gathering momentum, and the only difficulty I experienced was with enthusiasts who got to learn of the idea somehow or other, and wanted to advance their own patent ideas for an alternative to sinking block-ships.

I agreed to each of these ideas being briefly studied with one single exception: the Russians assured us that an effective breakwater could be created by bubbles of compressed air, but not, we very soon found, on anything approaching the scale that would be needed for our purposes. So compressed air was ruled out. All the more because it was undesirable for security reasons to bring the Russian Embassy into the secrets of the plan for *Overlord*.

It must have been about mid-June when Mountbatten wrote to General Morgan and suggested that C.O.H.Q. should organise and conduct a series of short courses for the benefit of senior Staff Officers and Junior Commanders who would be taking part in the invasion. The object would be to familiarise them with the facts of life and death in a great amphibious operation. He offered to make the Hollywood Hotel at Largs, which was already commissioned as a Combined Operations Training Centre, available for the whole time until D-Day.

Meanwhile he invited General Morgan, General Paget, Leigh-Mallory and myself to attend a meeting to discuss the project. In making this proposal I have always felt that Mountbatten was disappointed at the somewhat minor role being played by C.O.H.Q. in the planning of what was, one might say, the supreme end for which the Combined Operations Organisation had been created. He certainly had good cause for concern, for under the set-up agreed at Casablanca, nothing like enough use was being made of the immense amount of know-how available at Richmond Terrace.

Yet there were risks in his proposal: security was bound to be at some risk, and the danger of conflicting doctrine emerging from Norfolk House and C.O.H.Q. could not be ignored. Nevertheless, these risks could be, and indeed were, successfully overcome. However, General Paget was furious.

At first, he flatly refused to attend the meeting, but in the end, he was persuaded by Leigh-Mallory to come, and he offered to collect the Air Chief Marshal and myself from Norfolk House so that we could discuss the matter in his car, arrive together, sit together, and take a common line. He pointed out that the link which bound us together was simply that we already commanded many of the units which would be taking part, and consequently many of the officers who would do the courses.

In the car the General continued to denounce the whole project, and urged that we should turn it down flat. He felt that Freddie Morgan was unreliable on an issue of this nature because he had had too little experience of actual command. However, Leigh-Mallory maintained that much good might come of Mountbatten's idea, provided the first course got off on the right foot. He therefore suggested that he should speak on our behalf and welcome Mountbatten's initiative, after which he would propose that the first prototype course should be attended by us and our most senior Staff Officers.

Paget was taken aback by this astonishing suggestion and asked me to give my views before he replied. Thinking aloud, I suggested that if we had a gathering of Commanders-in-Chief, and Chiefs of Staff, it would be better to describe the deliberations as a "Conference" rather than as a course, and that the agenda should take the form of a number of short lectures by members of the Norfolk House Staff which would go chronologically through the whole operation, that is to say:

(i) Training and Training Areas.

(ii) Preliminary Operations (e.g., Interdiction and Minesweeping).

(iii) Assembly of the Naval Forces and Embarkation of the Troops.

(iv) Passage to France.

(v) Initial Assault.

(vi) "Follow-up" and "Build-up".

vii) Maintenance and Logistics pending the capture of major ports.

I argued that this could be done without disclosing the place or date of the landings, and further, that by conducting the conference on these lines, we should ensure that the C.O.H.Q. Staff, and also senior representatives of the Service Ministries, would be tuned in to the same wavelength. Each lecture could be followed by a short discussion, with Mountbatten in the Chair and winding up.

We remained sitting in the General's car at the entrance to Richmond Terrace while all this was discussed and agreed, and we arrived a little late for the meeting! When Mountbatten heard our suggestions, he at once agreed with them with enthusiasm and promised his full support. Freddie Morgan seemed a little bewildered at the turn events were taking, but he also promised full support. He then slightly disturbed some of us by adding that there could be no risk to security since no conclusions had yet been reached regarding the date and place of the landings. I wondered at the time whether he fully realised the extent to which we were now committed, and having since read his book, I realise that he did not.

The conference was an unqualified success and was indeed a landmark on the way to invasion. Admiral Little agreed to attend himself and proved a tower of strength. Apart from being the Naval Commander-in-Chief (Designate), he was easily the most senior and the most experienced officer present. I cannot now recall the number of Commanders-in-Chief who attended, or how many Sea Lords and members of the Army and Air Councils. Not without cause, the gathering was at once nicknamed "The Field of the Cloth of Gold".

From my own Norfolk House Staff came Captain Mansergh, and Captain Egerton, and also Captain Hutchings of the United States Navy. We travelled north in a special train, which we boarded after dinner on Sunday, 27 June. The conference lasted all day on 28 and 29 June, throughout the forenoon of 30 June and 1 July.

Perhaps this is the moment for me to describe the role played by Admiral Little at this period. He was, of course, my Administrative Chief in my "Force J" capacity, but operationally I came under the Chief of Combined Operations and the Admiralty. As Commander-in-Chief (Designate) for *Overlord*, he instructed me to keep him broadly in the picture about operational planning, but he did not wish to intervene unless I needed his support. On the other hand, I dealt only through him in all matters which involved the Naval Chain of Command.

During the *Rattle* Conference (as this gathering at Largs came to be called), Admiral Little had a splendid way of dealing with the legions of brigadiers who attended, and were fond of intervening in a dramatic way whenever their advice was overruled. In such cases they would say 'I can accept no further responsibility for the operation!'

'But Brigadier,' Sir Charles would reply, 'nobody is asking you to accept any responsibility. Our orders are to make the best possible plan. If you feel you can make a better one without exceeding the available forces, please let us hear about it. But responsibility for carrying out the plan will rest with the Combined Chiefs of Staff in Washington, together with Mr Churchill and the President.'

Unlike most conferences of this sort, several important decisions were taken. The first concerned training areas. I had already given much thought to this problem and discussed it with the naval authorities who would be affected, and also with the C.O.H.Q. Staff. The problem was to find suitable groups of harbours from which the new Naval Assault Forces could be exercised, and in whose area the divisions to be associated with each Force could be accommodated.

"Force J" already occupied the whole of the Portsmouth Command from Weymouth and Portland to Dover. It remained to make provision for four British Assault Forces and two American: that is to say four Naval Assault Forces in all, two of which were to be complete with the assault ships and assault landing craft, not forgetting the necessary support craft which would be committed to the initial assault, while the other two, which only being required for the follow-up on D-Day, would need no support craft and could be made up of tank landing craft, tank landing ships, and infantry landing craft.

After much discussion with the Americans, we were agreed that the American Assault Force should be based at Plymouth and use the harbours in the Plymouth Command. The American follow-up force would include, I learned, no landing craft, but only landing ships. This being so, it was agreed to base it in the Milford Haven area where there are magnificent harbours, but with Atlantic weather immediately outside them which would be too much for small landing craft.

To find room for the new British Assault Forces was less easy. At first sight it was tempting to use the Clyde Estuary and the area already used for ab initio amphibious training. However, the Combined Operations Command was understandably reluctant to accept a large influx of landing craft at the moment when the capacity of sea lochs and beaches would be stretched to their limits with the commissioning, trials and training for newly completed landing craft coming forward from the building yards. Moreover, the sea and beach conditions in south-west Scotland bore no relation whatsoever to those that would be met in the Channel. Accordingly, I suggested that "Force S" (the name given to the Force being formed to land the second British Assault Division) should be based at Invergordon and should use the Cromarty Firth as a training area, with the Naval dockyard at Rosyth as its principal maintenance base.

The other British Naval Follow-Up Force could then be based at Harwich and use that area for training. The question of training areas came up at the first session of the *Rattle* Conference, and I was asked to explain what the Navy had in mind. I did so, and was able to say that the British and American Naval authorities were in agreement. But I fortunately added that all must be subject to the agreement of the soldiers, since it was desirable, if not necessary, that each of the five divisions to be landed on D-Day should exercise with the Naval Assault Force that would be carrying them.

Consequently, these divisions ought to train in roughly the same areas as their Naval counterparts. General Puget immediately rose and expressed his vehement opposition to my proposals. Why must the Navy choose areas where there was no accommodation for troops on anything like the scale visualised? I replied that it was not really the Navy who had chosen the areas, but rather God when he sited the harbours and landing beaches round the Kingdom. It was agreed to remit the problem to a small group of those officers most directly concerned which would meet after dinner that night.

Accordingly, Admiral Little, Mountbatten, Leigh-Mallory and a number of the senior C.O.H.Q. Staff Officers, met at about 22.00 hours, only to be told that Paget had not yet made up his mind whether to come himself. So, we waited, and eventually he joined us at about midnight. Admiral Little began by repeating what I had said about the inevitability of the Naval choice. He added that the Admiralty and C.O.H.Q had been preparing for this particular contingency for over a year, and that we all supposed the War Office had been doing the same. However, he said it half in fun, and within an hour everything had been agreed.

I felt at the time, and still believe, that the wide dispersal of training areas round the United Kingdom served a secondary purpose in deceiving the enemy. Month after month the Germans must have become accustomed to receiving intelligence reports of intense amphibious training round our coast, and they must have speculated upon the objectives of each concentration of landing craft. To the German General Staff untrammelled as it was by much Naval knowledge, our forces in the Central Channel area must have seemed a threat to the coast from the Pas-de-Calais to the Cherbourg Peninsula. The force concentrated in the Plymouth area was clearly destined for Brittany, while the assembly of landing ships at Milford Haven posed a threat to the French Atlantic ports. What of the amphibious force at Cromarty and Rosyth?

Clearly its ships and craft were destined to land in southern Norway and Denmark, while the concentration in the Harwich area threatened the Low Countries. True, all these forces would have to converge and concentrate in one huge assembly in the Solent area, but this would only happen a matter of days before the invasion. Meanwhile the picture of widely dispersed forces would have become ingrained in the German mind from the study of intelligence reports for months on end, and elderly men are slow to discard mental pictures which have built up slowly.

The second matter which sticks in my mind about the *Rattle* Conference is the reception given to my proposal for an artificial port. General Brownjohn and I agreed to bring this up during the session devoted to logistics and the build-up. He opened with a talk about what would be involved in terms of men, vehicles, ammunition, petrol and stores during the first twelve weeks or so after D-Day. All this, he explained, would have to be landed over open beaches before we could be sure of having a major port. The faces of our distinguished audience were a study in gloom and scepticism as the tale unfolded. He then asked me to intervene and explain what we had in mind to ease the problem.

After referring to my own misgivings about over-reliance on the beaches, I disclosed our intention to establish a large area of artificially sheltered water by means of block-ships. I went on to say that if better and cheaper ways of making transportable breakwaters could be devised, we were wide open to suggestions. Initially I emphasised that the artificial harbour must be regarded as a principal requisite to our plans, both as an insurance against a prolonged spell of unseasonable northerly weather, and also against the beach surfaces breaking up as a result of repeated strandings of tank landing ships and coasters.

As soon as I sat down, General Paget rose to say that, if an artificial harbour was indeed technically feasible, a great weight of anxiety had been lifted from his mind, and for the first time he would take the operation seriously. Several senior officers of all three Services spoke in the same vein and someone from the Ministry of Shipping confirmed that the block-ships could and would be made available, although the Minister (Lord Leathers) would naturally prefer that some other method should be used.

After dinner the same evening, I saw Mountbatten alone, and asked whether he would agree to Sir Harold Wernher moving to Norfolk House to strengthen my staff and to co-ordinate the work of preparation for the artificial harbours. I pointed out that the work for which Sir Harold had originally been appointed to C.O.H.Q. was by now nearly complete, and that he would be the ideal man for this new task. It must have been a wrench for Mountbatten to lose Sir Harold's services. Nevertheless, he magnanimously agreed almost at once.

On the following day we had a final session at which Mountbatten wound up, and was followed by a free for all discussion. It was in the course of this discussion that Lieutenant General Bucknall of the 1st Corps, made rather a dramatic intervention. He expressed surprise that we still planned for the traditional tactics that had always been adopted for an assault landing, namely that a wave of infantry should approach under cover of darkness and be landed at first light with the object of securing the beaches.

After this they would be followed by armour and S.P. Artillery (i.e., self-propelled), which would pass through the infantry and advance inland. General Bucknall pointed out that these tactics had nearly always failed for the simple reason that if the beaches were resolutely held, the unfortunate infantry seldom succeeded in securing them but were pinned down, thus making the landing of the armour and artillery exceedingly hazardous. This is what had happened at Dieppe, and more recently it had happened again in Italy. He did not believe that the solution lay in stepping up the supporting fire, desirable though that might be on other grounds. Surely, he argued, the first wave of troops on an assault on a defended beach should be an integrated assault of all arms. First should come the Flail tanks to clear paths through the enemy minefields, each should be closely followed by a battle tank, which in its turn should be accompanied by the appropriate unit of infantry, say a platoon or section. Then should follow a suitable mix of all arms dependent on the nature of the terrain and the forces available.

It was apparent that the General's remarks commanded wide support among the more senior generals present, including General Anderson, fresh from his triumphs in Africa. Admiral Little therefore rose, and, after saying that he did not feel qualified to express an opinion on what seemed primarily a matter for the soldiers, he went on to assure General Bucknall that his ideas would be carefully explored by the Navy. Meanwhile, he asked me whether I would like to comment then

114

and there. I seized the opportunity as it was unlikely that so influential an audience would be assembled together again before the invasion actually took place.

I began by welcoming General Bucknall's ideas in the same way, and for the same reason, that General Paget had welcomed the artificial harbour idea, which had been put forward the day before. In particular I agreed that no amount of increased supporting fire would of itself ensure that the infantry could capture the beaches. Yet it was a hard fact that the great fleets of landing ships and landing craft that had been constructed by America and Britain had been designed and planned on the assumption that infantry embarked in small L.C.A. would land first, followed in due course by armour and artillery carried in tank landing craft. These tank landing craft proceed on their passage in big formations, whose best speed was perhaps 7 knots or less.

In contrast the infantry crossed in "Infantry Assault Ships" at a speed of at least 15 knots until they were 12 miles from their objectives, where they lowered their L.C.A. with the troops on board and completed their journey at perhaps 5 knots. To carry out General Bucknall's tactics one really needed a different type of assault craft, with good armour protection designed to carry two or three tanks, an assembly of S.P. Artillery with, say, a platoon of Infantry. It was now too late to construct such craft. The alternative, of using the craft which we had in fact got to use, was to work out a Naval manoeuvre whereby great numbers of assault ships could rendezvous with several squadrons of tank landing craft and then lower their L.C.A.s. in such positions and formations that the tank landing craft would overtake them and proceed inshore in close company with the particular L.C.A. carrying the infantry with whom the tanks they were carrying were to land.

I said that, while I was confident that the deployment to achieve all this could be evolved, it would call for quite different training to that which prevailed at present, and that this training would take months of hard work to perfect. The decision must therefore be incorporated in our outline plan, which was due to be completed by mid-August. Furthermore, I felt quite sure that the elaborate deployment which I visualised as being necessary could only be carried out in daylight. From my experience at Dieppe, I felt confident that daylight landings would be feasible. I therefore said that my first reaction to General Bucknall's idea was favourable.

Leigh-Mallory followed me and said that he enthusiastically welcomed the idea of landing in daylight. By doing so we should at least enable the R.A.F. to give proper and effective support to the Army at the most critical moment of the invasion, namely immediately after the troops were ashore. He agreed with me that Dieppe had shown that with air superiority the landing craft would be given effective protection from enemy bombers during their slow run into the beaches.

Although no formal decision was made at the time, Leigh-Mallory and I were from that moment completely sold on these new tactics, and General Paget was most decidedly in favour provided the Navy could cope with the complex deployment that would be involved.

I promised I would have the answer to this one way or the other before the end of September. Mountbatten was less decided, and as the more senior of the officers responsible for Combined Operation Training, thought I had under-estimated the time it would take to re-train the young Naval landing craft officers in what had hitherto been the foundation of their tactical training. However, he was wholly in favour of "Force J" testing the new techniques as soon as I was back at Cowes.

After luncheon I had a long tête-à-tête with General Bucknall to make sure that I had correctly interpretated his ideas. After that I flew back to London in a rather ropey U.S. transport aircraft in company with General McNaughton, General Morgan and others. The U.S. Army Air Force crew were all first-generation immigrants from Italy, and they said they were tickled to death to find that they had a cargo of senior officers. They warned us that the Pilot and Co-Pilot were very inexperienced, and that all of them had divided loyalties in proof of which numerous snapshots were handed round showing brothers and uncles in gorgeous Italian uniforms, both Army and Air Force. Before we left the aircraft, and amidst uproarious laughter, they warmly embraced us all, partly I felt sure because they knew we should be so embarrassed.

For the remaining weeks of my time at Norfolk House we were kept hard at work dotting the i's and crossing the t's of the outline plan, and also in preparing outline plans for one subsidiary and one alternative operation.

The subsidiary operation, which bore the code-name of *Starkey*, was only a large-scale feint landing in the Pas-de-Calais area to be carried out in September so as to synchronise with a projected landing in Italy well to the rear of the present front in the toe of Italy. In the event that landing was at Salerno, but I do not know whether this had been decided upon at the time we were told to plan the feint in July 1943. The prime object was to draw some of the German fighter squadrons away from Italy to airfields to the north-east of Paris.

For this reason, *Starkey* would be effective only if preparations were reasonably visible and were to occupy some days. A splendid opportunity for achieving this was afforded by the necessity for extensive minesweeping before large forces of landing ships and landing craft could safely operate outside our own coastal waters in the Pas-de-Calais area.

The principal Naval Force taking part could only be "Force J", and both Leigh-Mallory and I (who were to be in joint command) felt at first that we could more conveniently do the planning from Stanmore and Cowes respectively. However, I soon changed my mind, as, when acting in the name of COSSAC, other authorities, such as the Admiralty, the Ministry of Shipping, and the Home Forces Command, were far more ready to meet one's demand than I had ever found them before. As things turned out, the operation was more worthwhile than I had expected. It is described in more detail in the next chapter.

The other operation, code-name *Rankin*, was planned to meet the contingency of a German collapse in 1944. As there were no indications in the summer of 1943 that this was in the least likely to occur, I am bound to say that I grudged the time we spent on *Rankin*. Not so General Morgan, who was fascinated by its political overtones.

These arose because the plan for *Rankin* necessitated assumptions being made concerning the zones in Germany that would be occupied by the various Allied Powers. I never knew at the time the extent to which these zones were agreed by the Foreign Office, or indeed by the Russian Government. But I do recall that when I made a great fuss about Denmark being included in the Russian Zone, there seemed little difficulty in getting this changed.

But there was still some important and controversial detail to be written into the *Overlord* plan. Among the most emotive of these details was the provision to be made for casualties. It had already been accepted that some of our available tank landing ships must be converted for use as hospital ships to bring wounded men back to the U.K. in reasonable comfort. Sometime during July, Bob Mansergh drew my attention to the fact that so many tank landing ships were being demanded for this purpose that we should not have enough left to carry out the operation!

The pace was being set by the Americans, who had a small team of high calibre Staff Officers working exclusively on the casualty problem. Captain Hutchings told me that the reason why their demands were set so high was simply that the number of casualties they had been instructed to cater for was so astronomic. It appeared that the authority responsible for this was a civil bureau in Washington responsible to the President direct and its word was Law. Captain Hutchings explained that, only if we could substantiate a pretty strong case for reducing the Bureau's estimate of 50% casualties among all the troops who landed on D-Day should we be able to reduce the number of conversions to hospital ships.

For a couple of days, it looked as if the whole of our plan would be shipwrecked on this one issue. Then, after thinking it over, I suggested an entirely new approach: what would be the highest percentage of casualties day by day during, say, the first week after D-Day, that we could sustain without being forced to abandon the operation and withdraw? Surely there could be no point in making provision for a higher rate than this, because, if the operation had to be abandoned, the responsibility for caring for the wounded would rest with the Germans, and in any case the wounded could not be sent back to England. This argument appealed to the Americans, and left us with substantially fewer casualties to cater for than had previously been postulated.

Another vital problem was the scale, and probable effect, that the R.A.F. and U.S.A.A.F. could reasonably achieve by interdiction in the days leading up to D-Day. The Army was particularly anxious that as many as possible of the bridges over the Seine should be destroyed. Leigh-Mallory was equally anxious that the danger of over-optimism should be avoided, and his estimates were deliberately rather gloomy. In the event, the R.A.F. far exceeded what had come to be accepted, and if I remember rightly, nearly all the Seine crossings were written off.

The artificial port also reared its head again. Almost at the last moment Captain Hutchings asked me if I had heard the latest! 'Our Army boys,' he told me, 'are determined to have a port of their own off the Omaha and Utah beaches'. I protested that this was a technical impossibility as there was no convenient shoal water on which to sink blockships or caissons. Moreover, the U.S. beaches were better sheltered, except from a north-easterly gale. 'I have told them all that,' he said, 'but they have set their hearts on an artificial harbour of their own – almost as if it were a status symbol – they will have their way whatever you or I say, so we might as well string along with them'. I am afraid this is what we did, with predictable but tragic consequences.

By 20 July, the outline plan for *Overlord* was complete, and I spent almost the whole day together with Bob Mansergh and Brian Egerton, going through the plan with Admiral Little. The Admiral, with his great experience and meticulous eye for detail, was most helpful and played, as it were, the role of long-stop. By this date my successor as Chief of Staff (X) had been nominated in the person of Rear Admiral

George Creasy, (later Admiral of the Fleet Sir George Creasy). He had been promoted to Rear Admiral in the summer and was still serving as Flag Captain to the Commander-in-Chief, Home Fleet (Admiral Fraser), in command of H.M.S. *Duke of York*.

Accordingly, on 21 July, accompanied only by my Flag Lieutenant, I flew to Hatston in the Orkneys, and thence by boat to the *Duke of York* where, after dining with the Commander-in-Chief, I devoted the evening and half the night to turning over to Admiral Creasy. This was necessary because he was unable to join the Norfolk House Staff before 16 August, by which date it seemed that either I should be en-route for the Quebec Conference, or in the throes of the opening moves for Operation *Starkey*.

These alternatives confronted me with a dilemma. The Quebec Conference, to be attended by the Combined Chiefs of Staff, the President and the Prime Minister, was to be the forum before which General Morgan was to lay our plan for *Overlord*. I naturally wished to be present so as to be able to explain, and where necessary defend, the Naval aspects of the plan, including the artificial harbour. In particular I wanted to resolve one mis-giving which I had felt ever since I had proposed this harbour. Could we be sure that it would not silt up in a matter of weeks? Only harbour experts could answer this question, and only the heads of the two Governments could quickly call upon their services because the leading authorities in the world were at that moment working in the Far Eastern Theatre.

On the other hand, I had no doubt that Bob Mansergh could perfectly well take my place at Quebec, or alternatively, David Luce was perfectly able to direct Operation *Starkey* if I went to Quebec. In the end the matter was settled for me, because Admiral Little, supported by the Admiralty, insisted that I should remain in England to command *Starkey*.

It only remained for me to make my farewells and leave Norfolk House to return to Cowes. Accordingly, after spending most of 16 August completing my turning over to George Creasy (including turning over No.33 Eaton Terrace) I gave a farewell cocktail party and returned by car and boat to Cowes, arriving late.

Looking back on this interlude at Norfolk House, I am bound to say that the curious system which had been evolved at the Casablanca Conference of entrusting the planning of *Overlord* to a large staff working under Chiefs of Staff, to Commanders-in-Chief yet to be appointed, had worked better than anyone had had the right to expect. Why was it that we succeeded in producing a workable outline plan after the efforts of so many distinguished groups during the preceding eighteen months had run into the sands? I think the reason was two-fold: Firstly, the precise wording of the directive under which we worked did not allow nervous or self-important "G.2s" to down tools at regular intervals on the ground that they could accept no further responsibility. The second and more important reason was the presence among the staff at Norfolk House of senior officers who were not merely Staff Officers, but who also held command over some of the forces that would be committed to *Overlord*.

Among these I would include General Paget himself, because although it was known that he would relinquish command of the 21st Army Group before the invasion was launched, and although he held no formal position in the COSSAC "set-up", he none the less contrived to keep in close touch with what was being thought and planned at Norfolk House. The same, and even more so, can be said of Mountbatten.

In short, the lesson that I learned from my three months at Norfolk House is that every big planning staff should be leavened by a few officers in the Line of Command who know that in due course they will be called upon to play an active part in the execution of the plans on which they are working.

Chapter 7

OPERATION STARKEY

On my return to Force "J" in August, we had the advantage of being able to train and exercise with the object of carrying out a specific plan, with which, needless to say, I was fully familiar. We also had a number of immediate tasks to be carried out before the end of 1943. The first of these was to carry out a large-scale feint operation in the Strait of Dover, which was known as Operation *Starkey*, which had been recommended by the Joint Staff at Norfolk House, and had been approved by the Prime Minister.

It could be argued that *Starkey* was intended as an economical substitute for *Constellation*, but this would only be a half truth. To begin with, the capture of Sicily had been completed well before *Starkey* was due to begin. *Starkey* was intended to give the impression that a large-scale landing was imminent in the Pas-de-Calais area and thus to draw the German fighter strength away from the Italian theatre and back to north-east France and the Low Countries. The climax of the feint was timed to co-ordinate with the Salerno landings in Italy. It was further hoped that a great air battle would be brought about as this climax was reached, and that the Luftwaffe would suffer another crippling blow, as had happened at Dieppe. Briefly the plan was as follows.

On 23 August I shifted my Pennant to M.G.B. 312 and proceeded in company with two other M.G.B.s. to Dover, arriving at tea-time. Meanwhile, the operational part of my staff and key members of the Secretariat proceeded in what I can only describe as a "motorcade" to Dover, where a sizeable house had been taken to house me and my staff until *Starkey* was over.

The following week we devoted to meetings and visits preparatory to the operation. Although no troops would be landed it was intended to embark a substantial force of Army anti-aircraft units, both to swell the volume of A.A. fire, and help the illusion that the ships and landing craft taking part were loaded for an assault should they be photographed from the air.

The operation proper began on 31 August with three days of continuous minesweeping for which we had three flotillas of ocean-going minesweepers. By this time the Strait of Dover was deemed to be cleared of mines up to within 9 miles of the French coast. By then it was 6 September, and the ships taking part in the operation should have sailed that evening. They comprised about twelve infantry assault ships, approximately 100 tank landing craft, approximately thirty large infantry landing craft, plus all the available small infantry landing craft and six large infantry support craft. For escort duties there were eight or nine destroyers, and all available steam and motor gunboats. It was not intended that all these ships and craft should enter Dover, but rather in the main they should be routed close to Dover and then alter course as if they were making for the beaches in the Fécamp area, that is to say a few miles to the south and west of Boulogne.

However, much to the annoyance of Leigh-Mallory and myself, the operation was twice postponed, without reference to either of us. Why, I never found out for certain, but have always assumed that it was on account of last-minute postponements of the Salerno Landings. Be that as it may, the 48-hour delay confronted me with a dilemma. There was reason to suspect that the Germans were laying new mines in the area which had been swept, and we could not afford needlessly to hazard the landing ships and craft that were taking part in the feint since all were needed for the invasion in eight or nine months' time. Neither did we want to expose the minesweepers to undue risk. So far, they had led a charmed life.

It was estimated that the enemy had over 100 guns of 12" calibre and above mounted in the Calais/Boulogne area and capable of covering the area that had been swept. The weather had been perfect, with extreme visibility and, although there had been long periods of heavy fire during which the noise had been like the Battle of Trafalgar, only one minesweeper had been hit, and only one man killed.

For our defence we had relied on smoke screens, backed up by radar jamming. The smoke was laid mostly by coastal craft and landing craft, whose movements I directed from M.G.B. 312. If a screen was urgently required at a moment when no smoke craft were on hand, I could call on Leigh-Mallory, who maintained two squadrons of smoke making "Bostons" "at call". The radar jamming was carried out from specially equipped trailers towed by a form of Land Rover along the coast road that runs between Dover and Folkstone and on to Dungeness. For the jamming to be effective, the trailers had to keep the minesweeping flotilla they were protecting in transit with the battery which was firing at them.

Some doubt had been expressed before the operation on how effective this form of protection would prove. In the event it was a triumphant success, albeit at the cost of more "C.S." smoke than had ever before been used in a single operation, and with the help of some of the most brilliant radar experts in the country.

Indeed, Operation *Starkey* cleared up one important question which the Admiralty had raised about the Naval part of the plan for the invasion. In making this plan I had assumed that it would be possible to make at least a limited use of the Port of London for troop transports and store ships once a beach head had been established. This meant that these vessels must be routed through the Strait of Dover long before the Channel ports could be expected to be in our hands. *Starkey* established beyond doubt that, with suitable precautions, this would be possible.

For the final phase of *Starkey*, all the landing ships and landing craft were sailed from the Solent Ports, and from Newhaven, on 8 September, to proceed up-Channel as far as Dover, where they shaped course for Fécamp. Some thirty tank landing craft actually entered Dover Harbour in order to practice loading with tanks, to test the suitability of the new loading hards which had recently been constructed inside the harbour.

I watched this loading procedure with growing anger. Tank landing craft are difficult and unwieldy to handle. If there are ten to be loaded from each hard – as in this instance – they normally proceed in circles while waiting to go alongside, and it is important that as each craft completes loading and casts off, the one most favourably placed for going alongside should be the next to load. Each craft then assumes a "Fleet Number", the first to load being No.1, and the last No.10. These numbers are displayed on small boards which are fitted in brackets on the side of the bridge, and these numbers remain unchanged until the craft beach at their objective.

It is essential that the Army should know the sequence from left to right in which the tanks carried in each craft will be beached. But it does not matter in the least which tanks or troops are embarked in any particular landing craft so long as its position in the formation at the time of beaching is known. In other words, the permanent official number of an L.C.T. may be No.1053, but all that matters to the Army is that it will sail, say, as Fleet No.6 in the 4th Flotilla of "E" Squadron.

We had great difficulty in persuading the Senior "Movements" Officers on the staff at Norfolk House that this was so, and that any attempt to make a flotilla, numbering perhaps ten craft, come alongside in a pre-ordained sequence could and would involve a delay of anything up to two hours or more. When I walked down to Dover Harbour in the early hours of 9 September, I found a scene of some confusion, with a great deal of yelling through megaphones, and with little progress having been made with loading the craft. On remonstrating with their senior officer, I was told that a Lieutenant Colonel from the staff of South Eastern Army Command was insisting that the craft must come alongside in a particular sequence.

This turned out to be a "Movements" Officer, and I turned on him in fury and explained in suitable nautical language why he was causing so much delay. He did not seem unduly perturbed and said in reply that this was the first time he had understood the reason for the Naval Fleet numbering system, after which he became most helpful. (Three weeks later he arrived in my office at Cowes and reported that he was under orders to join my staff. By this means "Force J" acquired a "Movements" Officer of its own, qualified and authorised to move anything up to an entire Army – an enormous convenience when really large-scale exercises had to be carried out as the invasion date approached).

After this encounter I embarked in H.M.S. *Albrighton*, which proceeded to join the main Force in its passage towards Fécamp. A novelty had been installed in the *Albrighton* in the form of a direct and "scrambled" V.H.F. link between Fighter Command Headquarters and the ship, on which Leigh-Mallory and I could talk as easily as on a good telephone line. As we approached the enemy coast, the Air Chief Marshal told me that his intelligence indicated that since the minesweeping had started the Germans had re-deployed two-thirds of their total fighter strength in Italy to airfields north-east of Paris, and that he felt that this in itself had justified the time and the risks that had been taken with *Starkey*.

But our monitoring service, which could listen in to chatter between young German officers in command of the heavy gun batteries, showed that the German High Command were most suspicious that the fleet of landing craft approaching them were engaged in a feint. Leigh-Mallory also told me that repeated orders were being issued to the main German fighter bases forbidding any aircraft to take off until British troops had actually been seen to land. He explained that he, too, was faced with a dilemma. If he overdid the air cover provided over the ships and craft, it was unlikely that the Luftwaffe would dare to engage. Equally, if the aircover was unduly light, a successful fighter bomber attack might destroy a number of ships in a matter of minutes. Actually, he kept some eight fighter squadrons in the air above us, and these proved too much for the Luftwaffe to go for. On the other hand, the German military command did eventually authorise the commanders of the heavy batteries to open fire, which they proceeded to do when we were some 25,000 yards from them. The sound effects were impressive, but the results were nil.

The German decision to allow heavy guns to fire was helpful to us in one way. As one part of the plan, we had available some seventy American Flying Fortresses waiting to take off with heavy fighter escort in order to carry out precision bombing of the guns. So long as these guns were firing, they were easy to identify, but they were well camouflaged and the American air crews found them difficult to see when no firing was taking place. As a result of the firing, a number of heavy batteries were reported to have been destroyed.

One final feature of the feint should be mentioned. A sizeable convoy of some sixty ocean-going merchant vessels passed through the central Channel at dawn, and followed the coastal route to Dover, where it, too, turned southwards towards Fécamp. Its course was reversed at the same time as the leading landing ships and craft turned back when some 18 or 19,000 yards from Fécamp.

This was the first time since the Fall of France that an ocean-going convoy had proceeded to the east further than Southampton, and it was hoped, and believed by some, that the sight of an ocean convoy coming right up-channel would convince the Germans that something serious was afoot. In point of fact, I doubted if it had any effect at all, as by this stage of the war it is unlikely that the Germans had many pilots left with the nautical knowledge to distinguish between ocean going vessels and large coasters.

All the ships and craft taking part in *Starkey* were safely back by the late afternoon of 9 September.

In retrospect, *Starkey* was perhaps of more importance than it seemed at the time. The limitations of the great batteries were exposed, and their threat cut down to size. It was thought that with proper precautions it was quite safe to route, and even to operate, valuable ships through and in the Strait of Dover. Secondly, it was shown that the enemy were unwilling to challenge our command in the air unless the Allied troops had actually been landed. It was also shown what strides in the training of landing ships and landing craft had been made since Dieppe. In *Starkey* we had a Naval force about three times as great as that at Dieppe, and even under the stress of heavy bombardment from the shore, there was no difficulty in handling them and in keeping them together in proper formation.

Finally, the minesweeping phase of the operation gave David Luce, Adrian Butler and myself three precious days at sea during which no-one could interrupt us, and we used this time to work out a new method of deployment with which to achieve the entirely novel "integrated landings", which it has now been decided to attempt on the Normandy beaches in a few months' time.

With the completion of Operation *Starkey*, only three urgent tasks remained for "Force J" which I wanted to carry out before the end of 1943. It was necessary to protect the deployment to which I have referred on a full assault-force scale: that is to say some fifteen flotillas of tank landing craft, numbering up to 150 craft all told, must be able to change from the formation in which they would make their passage to France (normally with flotillas in close double column disposed astern) to the formation in which they would make their final run-in to the beaches (that is to say with flotillas in close double column disposed abeam). While this change of formation was being executed, the whole tank landing craft force must rendezvous with the infantry assault ships near to the position where they would lower their L.C.A. so that these craft could take close station on the tank landing craft flotilla with which they were to beach.

The need to manoeuvre such large numbers of tank landing craft with precision and speed had not been foreseen before the *Rattle* Conference in the summer of 1943, and it presented a difficulty inasmuch as the range of speed of a typical tank landing craft was so small, perhaps from a minimum of 6 to a maximum of 8 knots, i.e., 2 knots. One had to look back to the seventeenth century to find a parallel. That is to say, to the days when fleets of fifty or sixty sailing ships were common. In those days the standard method was by means of "equal speed manoeuvres" and this continued to be a standard method right up to the First World War.

To take a simple example, if one wished to change formation from Line Ahead to Line Abreast, the Flag Ship would turn 90° to port or starboard, and the remaining ships would follow in succession until all were once more in Line Ahead but steering at right angles to the original course. The Admiral would then make a signal for all ships to turn together and resume the original course, by which time the Fleet would be in Line Abreast.

However, as the number of ships dwindled, and as the effective range of speed of warships increased (perhaps to 15 knots) it became more convenient to use "unequal speed manoeuvres". In this case, to change from Line Ahead to Line Abreast, the leading ship would reduce speed to, say, 10 knots, and those astern would increase perhaps to 25 knots and steer out to port or starboard, reducing speed as they came abeam of the leader. "Unequal speed manoeuvres" were liable to take longer to complete, but they needed less sea room, and called for less skill in ship handling. Yet, when I first came to sea in H.M.S. *Lion*, the Flag Ship of the Battle Cruiser Force, we normally had from fourteen to eighteen capital ships in company when proceeding on a routine sweep of the North Sea, and Sir William Pakenham, who was in command, loved to execute "equal speed manoeuvres" which he personally directed from our compass platform, entirely by eye, and with faultless judgment. Yet, "equal speed manoeuvres" were virtually dead by the time the Second World War broke out.

After deep thought I came to the conclusion that we must revive them in "Force J" because the conditions that had made them suitable in by-gone days had come again, so far as major landing craft were concerned. My staff thought that I had gone mad, and doubted whether we should ever teach the young R.N.S.V.R. officers who commanded landing craft to master them. But these young men at once became intensely interested, and grew quite adept. To watch the whole Force change its formation and deploy for an assault landing was an impressive sight, and inspired in me complete confidence of what would happen on D-Day.

The second task was to test our ability to land the "follow-up" brigades at the speed which had been assumed to be possible on the Normandy beaches. General Paget and his 21st Army Group Staff felt some doubt about this, partly because they suspected the efficiency of the new "waterproofing system" that had recently been evolved for all types of army vehicle, including tanks. The rate of landing over beaches was very sensitive to waterproofing failures, because any Army vehicle whose engine stalled as it left its landing craft to cross the water gap caused a disproportionate delay to the whole landing. This was particularly true when a landing was being made near low water on a rising tide. A stalled vehicle would then be quickly drowned and hidden under the sea as the water rose. Landing craft beaching with subsequent formations were liable to run aground on these submerged vehicles.

The invasion plan required that a complete Brigade Group should be landed on a front of about 1 mile, and that the beach and its approaches should be cleared for the next Brigade Group within a period of two hours. The exercise to test this was carried out on 20 September at East Wittering, where the beach gradient was similar to that of the Normandy beaches. The Brigade Group selected numbered 5,000 men and 850 vehicles, and, by coincidence, was commanded by one of David Luce's brothers. Some seventy-two tank landing craft, plus twelve L.C.I.(S) took part, and I watched from an M.L. Other spectators included Admiral Little, Sir George Creasey, who had succeeded me at Norfolk House, General Paget, and General Barker of the U.S. Army and one of the Norfolk House Staff.

One requirement of this exercise was that, in order to test the waterproofing, there should be 9" waves! General Paget was most keen on this and he came with me in the early hours of the morning of the 20th to watch two tank landing craft squadrons embark their vehicles. At 02.00 hours that morning there was a flat calm, and the General suggested that we must be prepared to repeat the exercise when there was more wind and sea, but we need not have worried: by 08.00 hours there was an on-shore wind of Force 6, and a heavy surf. The landing craft did their stuff in an impressive way.

The whole military force was ashore in one-and-a-half-hours and the beach and its approaches were cleared of landing craft in the same time. Only one tank landing craft broached-to and had to await the next tide. All the L.C.I.(S) had difficulty with the surf, but their powerful engines got them out of trouble. Four or five Army vehicles got stuck in the sand, but not, apparently, through any failure of the waterproofing.

Nevertheless, they could not be salved before the tide rose and submerged them. By the time it fell again they had vanished without trace, having been swallowed up in the sand. So far as I know they must be hidden under East Wittering beach to this day. Later in the forenoon I drove to London and spent the afternoon at an important meeting at Norfolk House. My feelings were of great relief since once again we had seen a remarkable vindication of a wearisome year of training.

It remained to carry out a full-scale divisional landing supported by live fire from 25-pounder guns and rockets, in which the whole of "Force J" was to participate, backed by some 500 landing craft allocated to the build-up phase of the landing. Originally the 3rd Division had been allocated to "Force J" for the actual invasion, but at the request of the Canadian Authorities, the 3rd Canadian Division (Major General Keller) had been substituted for sentimental reasons, in view of the association of "Force J" with Canadian Troops at Dieppe. Bearing in mind the awful losses suffered by the 2nd Canadian Division, I was deeply touched at this evidence of trust and friendliness.

Accordingly, in this first large-scale rehearsal the 3rd Canadian division was to be embarked for the assault landing. The plan was to assemble the whole force at Spithead and to sail round the Isle of Wight, and then proceed to the westward to Studland Bay, where there was a beach just large enough for a divisional landing, giving access to an Army "Firing Range" which "Force J" had taken over. The passage would have been roughly the same length as the passage to the Normandy beaches. A heavy concrete bunker had been built at the centre of the landing beach to accommodate V.I.P. spectators. There was no lack of these, and they included the First Sea Lord – by now Lord Cunningham – the Vice Chief of Naval Staff, and other senior Admiralty Officers.

The Army was represented by General Morgan from Norfolk House, General Paget, and other Generals of the 21st Army Group. General Crerar also came on behalf of the Canadian Army, and there was a small posse of American Generals. I myself embarked in an infantry assault ship called the *Isle of Thanet,* which had been specially fitted out at enormous cost as a temporary Headquarters Ship. Admiral Little embarked in her as well, but only as an observer. Leigh-Mallory came too, but this was his normal custom after he had become Commander in Chief of Fighter Command whenever "Force J" was carrying out a major exercise.

We also embarked a number of Junior Fighter Pilots: (ever since the Dieppe Raid we had received a party of about seventy of these boys once a fortnight. They came to see different types of landing craft and stayed at the Squadron Castle for drinks before leaving). By this means a warm bond of friendship had grown up between "Force J" and Fighter Command.

Reverting to Exercise *Pirate*, as it was called, the intention was that the exercise should continue for some 48 hours after the initial assault landing by the 3rd Canadian Division. The landing craft were then to return direct to Southampton and embark another division (the 47th, I think) and then return to Studland Bay and land them as if they were a follow-up division.

"D" Day for the exercises was Sunday, 17 October, and I embarked in the *Isle of Thanet* at Southampton on Saturday, 16 October. We were confronted on arrival on board with a most unfavourable weather forecast, which included the threat of a south-westerly gale. With the agreement of Leigh-Mallory and General Keller, I therefore decided to modify the plan, and sail the whole force westward through the Solent and pass out through the Needles Channel, thus being sure of sheltered waters for a few hours until daylight, and also greatly shortening the length of the passage to Studland Bay.

New orders were got out before noon, and the Force proceeded down harbour in the afternoon. It was not until I saw the astonishment of some of the old Combined Operations hands at our ability to change the plan and the route at such short notice that I realised how much the training of "Force J" had progressed.

The *Isle of Thanet* presented problems as a Headquarters Ship, not the least of which was that the Admiralty had not "commissioned" her, which meant that she flew the Red Ensign and was manned by a Merchant Navy crew. To legalise the presence of the officers who embarked in her, we all had to sign on as "supernumeries" and were paid 1d. per day. This went for myself, the Air Chief Marshal, General Keller and all the Staff Officers.

A further problem arose about my Broad Pennant, which had to be worn by the ship from which the senior officer was issuing Executive Orders. The Admiralty ruled that a flag or pennant could not be flown by a Red Ensign Ship, and suggested that a destroyer should be detailed to fly it, and to remain in very close company with the *Isle of Thanet*. Apparently, this had been done on more than one occasion in the Mediterranean. However, destroyers were as rare as gold in the Channel, and I could not possibly waste one of them on this task.

The *Isle of Thanet* being basically an assault ship, carried six assault landing craft, of which one was always turned in, and rendered unserviceable, for routine maintenance. These craft were manned by R.N.V.R. crews and were, of course, entitled to fly the White Ensign. Accordingly, I wore my Broad Pennant on a short flag staff which was fitted in whichever landing craft was hoisted in for maintenance. The Admiralty confirmed that this was lawful and would enable me to direct "Force J" from the *Isle of Thanet*. But the Admiralty never do things by half, and the Midshipman or Sub-Lieutenant who was in charge of the assault landing craft wearing my pennant was paid a substantial "Flag Captain's Allowance", which more than doubled his pay, with the result that the arrangement was highly popular with the boys.

Despite the last-minute change of plan, the exercise went off very well on the whole. We found that the westerly tidal stream in the vicinity of Yarmouth was too strong for any tank landing craft, which failed to hit off the gate through the anti-submarine nets which guarded the westerly end of the Solent, with precision. Any craft which had to make a last-minute alteration of course was swept into the net and caught and held until slack water. Some six tank landing craft became non-starters for this cause, and, as David Beatty signalled at the time, the scene at the net was rather like a gigantic trawling operation. We decided there and then that this net would have to be removed now that the landing craft were required to operate in such numbers, and that we must accept the risk of a U-boat entering the Solent via the Needles Channel.

Apart from this mishap, the initial Assault took place according to plan and appeared to be well executed. The covering fire from

25-pounder guns embarked in two flotillas of L.C.T. was reported by the V.I.P.s watching it from the shelter of the concrete bunker, to be particularly effective. The idea of making use of the 25-pounder guns landed in the initial assault to support the Infantry by fire from their craft during the final "run-in" had originated in the fertile mind of Commander Redvers Prior. He had begun to practise it in co-operation with local military units some time before "Force J" was created, and some months before the Dieppe raid.

It was highly popular with the Army because the ammunition expended during this particular training did not come out of their normal practice quota. The idea was to embark four or six guns in the hold of each craft where the guns' crews were protected by the hull of the craft, and given further protection by sandbag walls erected between each gun. The direction of the gunfire was controlled by steering the craft, and was the responsibility of the Captain of the L.C.T. The range set for the guns was governed by a simple old fashioned "Vickers Clock" which was kept set to the speed, measured in yards per minute, at which the L.C.T. flotillas were approaching the beach. Initial spotting corrections were needed to get the shells falling in the desired area, after which the guns' crews merely had to blaze away as fast as they could.

For Exercise *Pirate* we also had six rocket craft, which fired their entire output of rockets (6,600 in all) during the final "run-in". This tremendous volume of fire (because all the rockets landed within half a minute), was quite awe inspiring. It also involved a considerable risk whenever a full outfit of rockets was fired. Two or three invariably fell very short, probably as a result collisions in the air. Consequently, they fell among the landing craft going in ahead, and in every large-scale exercise there were likely to be two or three fatal casualties from this cause.

I am bound to say that this gave both me and my staff considerable uneasiness at the time, but the Army was adamant that the troops must be accustomed to going in underneath powerful support fire, as otherwise they feared that the troops would be almost as shocked as we hoped the Germans would be.

The whole of the assaulting division was ashore well before noon, and in addition a "Beach Battalion", an "R.A.F. Commando" and other maintenance troops had been landed together with their stores and vehicles by about 16.00 hours. This was the first full scale exercise in which these ancillary forces had been included. (They had, of course, been landed for exercises by themselves on a number of occasions before).

By the time all were ashore, the rocket craft and other support craft were on their way back to their bases, while all the tank landing craft and infantry landing craft were back in their Southampton area to embark the follow-up division. From my point of view there was little to see or to do once the 3rd Canadian Division were safely ashore, and the same went for the V.I.P.s watching from the shore. Some of them, including two members of the Board of Admiralty, came off to the *Isle of Thanet* at about noon and spent nearly an hour on board. They were shown round the Operations Room, and the general tactical plan for assault landing was explained to them, after which I signalled to the Principal Beach Master to send for an L.C.P. to collect them.

To my dismay he chose one of the "build-up" craft whose crew had only manned their boat for the first time some fourteen days before, and had only been in the Navy for perhaps ten to twelve weeks since being called up. So, I apologised in advance, but Admiral Little re-assured us and said he thought both the crew and the craft looked very smart, and so they did, in their brand new uniforms and in a brand new L.C.P.

As the craft drew near the gangway, a young seaman sprang up in her bows and grabbed a boat hook. 'There you are', said the Admiral, 'you see the bowman knows the proper drill and is going to bear her bows off as she comes alongside'. But the young man had other ideas. Using the boat hook to steady himself, he unbuttoned the flap of his bell bottom trousers and turning down wind, proceeded to relieve nature long and strongly, while the coxswain was left to hold on to the gangway.

Shortly afterwards I received an urgent message from St. Leger Moore at Cowes saying that my presence was urgently required. When I got to my office it transpired that there had been a mistake and accordingly, I returned to Studland Bay, overtaking three squadrons of L.C.T. laden with vehicles and armour of the follow-up division.

By this time, however, the weather had changed and it was blowing hard from the south-west, with the threat of a south-westerly gale. Accordingly, I stopped the exercise and ordered the tank landing craft to return at once to the Solent through the Needles Channel. It was only just in time; even so, most of the tank landing craft had been swept so far inshore that their Squadron Commanders boldly and wisely decided to make for Hurst Point, steering inside the shoals which ran north and south just to the west of Hurst Point. I told the Master of the *Isle of Thanet*, who was a grand old man well on in his sixties, to reduce speed and act like a sheep dog towards the tank landing craft.

Long before we reached the Needles, darkness had fallen. It was an exceptionally dark night, and the passage through the Channel with some seventy tank landing craft in what was by now a full gale was an anxious experience. The old Master was pessimistic: 'They're gonners, Sir, they're gonners' was all he said, and repeated it over and over again. However, to my relief, and I am bound to add, surprise, not one landing craft of any type was lost or damaged.

Thus concluded the first full scale exercise carried out before *Overlord*, and it only took one meeting with General Keller to decide on the further big exercises that needed to be carried out before "D" Day. Furthermore, we agreed that the first of these could wait until March 1944.

Meanwhile I was left with only routine administration coupled with V.I.P.s' visits to cope with. Administration had reached formidable proportions. "Force J" now totalled over 15,000 officers and men and was – so the First Sea Lord told me – the largest single administrative unit in the Navy. Its mere size presented problems and an "O" and "M" team who visited Cowes found that we averaged 1,200 "In" and 1,100 "Out" signals a day, and that we received and sent 3,000 letters a week.

If I wished to assemble all the officers, as, for example, for the post mortem on a big exercise like *Pirate*, it was necessary to borrow the largest cinema in Southampton for use as a hall. Moreover, as the only complete and trained assault force, not to mention the one which was geographically most accessible from London, we received an unending stream of visitors, most of whom were too exalted for anyone except myself to receive and entertain.

Of these, the most interesting and important was Field Marshal Smuts, Prime Minister of the Union. He was brought over from Portsmouth by Admiral Little on 29 October, and his arrival was preceded by a message from Mr Churchill instructing me that all the plans and special craft and weapons connected with *Overlord* could be discussed and shown to him.

Smuts was accompanied by a number of Staff Officers, plus, I think, his son. We lunched immediately after his arrival, and Admiral Little then returned to Portsmouth. David Luce and I then took the Field Marshal in a steam gunboat at full speed to the Needles Range, where a number of support craft were waiting to demonstrate their fire power. They included a rocket craft, and it had been intended that the rockets should be fired to the westward from a position just beyond Hurst Point. But the visibility was too low for this to be safe, so we decided instead to fire at the cliffs in Allum Bay. The noise, augmented by echo, was like a prolonged clap of thunder, and the cliffs were immediately hidden in a gigantic cloud of dust. As this subsided, it looked as if they had had a spring cleaning, and the famous-coloured sands showed up more brilliantly than anyone present had ever seen them before.

After returning to Cowes, Smuts asked whether he could speak to me privately, and we adjourned to my room in the Squadron Castle – just the three of us, the Field Marshal, David Luce and myself.

There followed one of the most interesting hours I have ever spent. After all, Smuts possessed perhaps the most brilliant and wide-ranging intellect of our time. A leading scientist in his own right, a lawyer of international repute, a great captain of war, and an equally revered statesman, all rolled into one. He wasted little time on the forthcoming invasion because, he explained, he was lukewarm in his support for the whole project.

'You are like a gambler', he told me. 'For practical purposes you have won the war already, and now you want to toss the enemy double or quits by launching the one operation which, if it fails, could rob you of victory'. 'But I see your mind is set', he added.

I explained that it did not lie with me to decide this great issue: I was there to do what I was told. 'Rubbish', he replied, 'if you were publicly to withdraw you support from *Overlord* it would never take place. If I were your age and commanded this magnificent force, I should embark a couple of divisions and sail at once for the Mediterranean where it could play a decisive role.'

David Luce interposed to point out that as the station-keeping speed of "Force J" as a whole was only 7 knots, we should be overtaken by a Police launch and brought back under arrest almost before we were out of sight of land. 'Well, drop a line to Mr Churchill explaining your intentions', he said. 'I will deliver it myself, and I am sure he would support you.'

Smuts then turned to South African problems, and he told me how much he had admired my great uncle (Sir Henry, and afterwards Lord Loch) who had been Governor of the Cape until a short time before the Jameson Raid. 'You cannot imagine,' he said, 'the veneration in which he was held by young liberal minded Boers like myself'. After explaining his deep forebodings about the future, he said: 'But one thing I beg you, never despair of my people. One day they will be transformed by a great surge of moral uplift. Be patient and do not interfere: there lies the path of true Statesmanship.'

Finally, he came to the future of Europe, and asked us whether we had thought much about the kind of Europe we should have to live in after the war. It would, he prophesised, be a Europe dominated by fear of Russia, overshadowed by the threat of world revolution to be imposed and organised by the mighty Russian Army. He went on to say that there need in fact be no fear, because the threat of Communism, backed as it would be by Russian military strength, would have the effect of uniting Western Europe as it has not been united since the Turkish and Moslem threat of the sixteenth century And yet the fear of Russia, and of Communism, which would be the mainspring of this new found unity, would persist thirty, sixty, or perhaps 100 years, and then one fine day the peoples of Western Europe would wake up and realise that the danger had passed, that the tide of Communism had receded leaving only a trail of slime behind.

'That', he went on, 'would be the moment of real danger: the danger that when no longer united by fear, the old animosities between the Western Powers would break out again, and that Europe and the civilisation which it had engendered would go down in irretrievable ruin in a Third Great Civil War.'

His message to my generation was, therefore, simple but urgent: there would be a limited time after the war was over during which the political and economic unity of Western Europe would be practical politics. But the time was limited, and if England, France and Germany failed to make use of it, their days would be numbered.

Smuts told me that this had been the theme of all the recent private talks he had had with Mr Churchill, and he had had no difficulty in convincing him. Shortly afterwards he made a speech in this country on similar lines, but precious little notice was taken of it. When in 1946 the great Churchill himself cried at Zurich 'Europe Unite', Continental Europe listened, but not the English – not in particular the so-called "Working Classes". When one reads in 1972 the humbug and poppycock preached by English Trade Union Leaders to their docile and dim-witted followers, one wonders whether they do not need the discipline of yet another terrible war to bring them to their senses.

Chapter 8

BACK TO SEA

By the time of this memorable visit by Smuts, my days with "Force J" were numbered. During most of the time I had been with Combined Operations I had been kept too busy to give much thought to my own position and career. However, my mind had been alerted to such trivialities shortly before I had left Norfolk House in August. General Morgan had warned me privately and in confidence that he had reason to believe that a high-level intrigue was going on to replace Admiral Little as the Naval Commander-in-Chief (Designate) by Admiral Ramsay.

I was as deeply shocked as the General because, like him, I had been brought up to believe that ever since the days of the formidable Lord Fisher, intrigue was unknown in the Royal Navy. On thinking it over, however, I felt sure that neither Sir Charles nor I would be displaced so long as Dudley Pound remained First Sea Lord. Yet there were serious doubts as to whether the old Admiral's health would stand the immense strain to which it was exposed much longer.

At about the same time, I had spent a short weekend at the Squadron Castle with General Paget, Leigh-Mallory and Freddie Morgan himself as my guests. During luncheon on the day of our arrival, David Luce told me that his patience was becoming exhausted by the arrogant and incompetent youths who were being supplied to us as Commanding Officers of Tank Landing Craft Flotillas. They were appointments for which a Lieutenant Commander was required, but we were receiving immensely young Acting Lieutenant Commanders of the Combined Operations branch of the R.N.S.V.R. (In fact, I had recently met one of these "whiz-kids" who told me that less than eighteen months previously he had been an Ordinary Seaman!)

David Luce asked me why we could not have fairly senior regular Lieutenants of the Royal Navy serving as Acting Lieutenant

Commanders. Both General Paget and Leigh-Mallory then intervened to say that they felt sure the Admiralty would never agree, because such a policy might upset the "Career Structure" of the Navy which, they rather unkindly added, was of more concern to the Sea Lords than winning the war. Although this was said in fun, there was just sufficient germ of truth in it to make me think about what was going to happen to myself. Operation *Starkey*, which came shortly afterwards, with its long periods at sea with the minesweepers, gave me more time for reflection at a moment when I was becoming more and more aware of the magnitude of the "Force J" Command.

The more I thought about it, the more sure I felt that I should be superseded before *Overlord* took place. After all, "Force J" was by far the largest of the assault forces, and whoever commanded it in June would be holding the principal sea-going command in the greatest operation of the war, and would also have to act as the Senior Naval Officer Afloat in the British Sector. Yet even if the war went on for a year after we had landed in France, I should still be only half way up the Captains' List, and with the fame that success would have brought, it seemed unlikely that I should be regarded as employable again in the rank of Captain.

Retirement with a war service rank of Rear Admiral, and perhaps a monetary grant from Parliament, seemed a more likely fate. I therefore wrote privately to Admiral Little in this sense, pointing out that if I were to return to ordinary service, now would be the time for me to go, with over six months to run before *Overlord*, with "Force J" completely formed and three-quarters of the way to being completely trained.

Alternatively, I suggested that a Vice Admiral should be appointed as Deputy Commander-in-Chief who would act as the Senior Naval Officer Afloat, leaving each Assault Force Commander concerned with only that part of the British Sector in which his own Force was landing troops. However, the Admiral told me that Dudley Pound wished for no changes to be made. Soon afterwards, Dudley Pound became gravely ill and died, being superseded by Admiral Cunningham.

On 22 October, Sir Charles Little called me on our private direct line late at night to say that his appointment as Naval Commander-in-Chief (Designate) for *Overlord* was being terminated, and that he was to be replaced by Admiral Ramsay. I was deeply grieved on his behalf, and also grieved because, successful though Admiral Ramsay had been in a limited sphere, he was not a man of the same calibre as Admiral Little, and his Mediterranean experience of amphibious warfare would have little relevance to the totally different conditions prevailing in the Channel, where strong tidal streams are a landing craft's principal enemy.

Despite bitter disappointment, Admiral Little behaved as anyone who knew him would have expected – with the utmost dignity.

On 27 October, the cruiser H.M.S. *Glasgow* came to Portsmouth to embark the ashes of Dudley Pound, and also of Lady Pound, who had pre-deceased him by a few months. The Admiralty had given precise orders about who should proceed to sea in H.M.S. *Glasgow* to attend the Committal Service. Only the Commander-in-Chief himself, Admiral Pipon (who was the Flag Officer-in-Charge at Southampton) and myself, went from Portsmouth Command, while Admiral Dalrymple Hamilton (at that time the Naval Secretary to the First Lord) and Lord Cunningham, the new First Sea Lord, came from the Admiralty.

There was a dead calm and very poor visibility, and the ship stopped just beyond the Nab Tower. The service was short, simple, and deeply moving, and attended only by the Officers I have named and a few Royal Marines. We were back alongside in time to have a late luncheon with Admiral Little. During our return to Portsmouth, Lord Cunningham drew me aside and said he wished to talk about my future. He then deployed the same arguments in favour of my return to General Service as those which I had already advanced myself. He added that he intended to pay me the compliment of appointing Britain's foremost Operational Vice Admiral as my successor, namely Sir Philip Vian. Furthermore, he would see that the command of a modern heavy cruiser was made available for me, despite the fact that "Force J" would also count as a sea command in my Record of Service. He went on to say that he had already had some most favourable comments on the morale and efficiency of "Force J", and I was not to be brow-beaten by Philip Vian into acquiescing to changes in the course of our turning over.

The following day I went to London to attend a long afternoon meeting at Norfolk House on the subject of assault tactics. Admiral Ramsay presided, and although most of those present were Naval Officers, Generals and Air Marshals were in good supply. Leigh-Mallory himself was not there, but he had sent a message to Ramsay to the effect that he agreed with my views.

It soon became clear that Admiral Ramsay, who had not heard of the plan for an integrated daylight landing before his appointment as Commander-in-Chief, was understandably reluctant to depart from the conventional tactics which had always been adopted hitherto. Apparently, Admiral Creasy (who had stayed on as his Chief of Staff) had been unable to convince him of the wisdom of the change. He now asked me, as the person responsible for accepting the new tactics on behalf of the Navy, to explain my reasons. I did this at some length and formed the opinion that opposition did not come so much from Admiral Ramsay himself as from those Officers of his staff whom he had brought from the Mediterranean. At the end of a long and tiring meeting, Admiral Ramsay announced a firm decision to stick to the new tactics; a decision which cannot have been easy for him to make, and for which I must admire him.

During the forenoon before this meeting, I had seen the Admiral privately and he confirmed that the First Sea Lord had told me the day before about Admiral Vian's nomination as my successor. He went on to press me to remain with the organisation as Admiral Vian's Chief of Staff. This did not appeal to me. It would not have been easy in the circumstances to continue as Chief of Staff where one had ruled as Commander for over a year. Moreover, neither Philip Vian nor I were easy people to work with, as both of us had strong wills and did not suffer fools gladly, and I suspected that Philip Vian, like myself, was apt to classify as a fool anyone who disagreed with him. However, I thought it prudent to ring up Dalrymple Hamilton and explain what had happened and seek his guidance. He promised to consult the First Sea Lord.

On my return to Cowes the following day, and just before Field Marshal Smuts arrived, Lord Cunningham rang up himself, and said that he thought the suggestion that I should stay on in a subordinate capacity was 'a most improper one' and I had acted quite rightly in refusing. His promise of a Cruiser command stood firm, and I should continue in the rank of Commodore 1st Class until I had actually assumed command.

My remaining days with "Force J" were taken up with receiving distinguished visitors, and a whole round of farewells. Admiral Vian arrived on 9 November and a signal from the Admiralty suggested that our turnover should be spread over a whole week. We both felt that this was unnecessary, and that two days would be ample. Vian told me that he liked to think and talk while he was walking, and so did I.

Accordingly, after introducing me to the staff, we had luncheon and then went for a fast three-hour walk. Much of our talk was about the staff, because he displayed the new broom's instinctive desire to replace any officer he did not know by someone with whom he had served before. In particular he did not relish St. Leger Moore as his Administrative Chief of Staff; nor like the idea of keeping the Administrative and Operational sides of the Naval Staff distinct. I said that St. Leger Moore, despite his having been so much my senior in years and rank, had served with me with complete loyalty, and with consistent efficiency.

As to how the staff was organised, he must judge for himself. He then suggested that David Luce was far too young to be Chief of Staff, and he mentioned a senior Captain for whom he had already applied. Did not I agree that this would be an improvement? I did not – and said so with such vigour that the formidable Sir Philip stopped dead in his tracks. An awful silence followed, and to my astonishment the Admiral said, 'Forget it. I will keep Luce.'

Another revealing thing happened late the same night. It was my custom to return to my office after dinner and stay until about midnight going through signals and letters that were outstanding. The Admiral said he would like to come with me and watch. I came to a signal which I could not follow and rang for the Secretary to explain what it was about. While this was going on, Vian looked at the signal and expresses great surprise when he saw that it was an "Out" signal – that is to say one made from the "Commodore Force J". 'You mean that you allow signals to be made in your name that you have not personally seen and approved?' he said. I explained that we averaged over 1,000 "Out" signals a day, and if I did not delegate, I should die.

Sir Philip was not in the least convinced, and said that he would not allow this to go on after he had taken over. On the following day I had to take Lord Chatfield round the Solent to see some of our bases and craft. Vian suggested that he should follow us round in my barge, accompanied by David Luce. This was a good idea, and when I finally got back to the Castle after landing Lord Chatfield at Portsmouth, I found Admiral Vian in buoyant spirits. He had been deeply impressed by the fact that every unit in "Force J" we had passed had piped and stood to attention as we went by. He explained that he had not been prepared for such discipline and vigilance.

I left "Force J" after breakfast on 11 November, after a farewell lunch given by the Post Captains of the Force at Lepe House. I then changed into Captain's uniform and drove to the Littles' house at Portsdown Hill, where I dined and spent the night before saying goodbye and going on leave. Two months later, I received a most charming letter from Sir Philip.

Full of praise for the state in which the Command had been turned over, he went on to say that he was kept working until between 2 and 3 in the morning for the first three weeks after I had left. He then persuaded the Admiralty that the Force was too big a command for a single Flag Officer, and should be split into two, with himself in Operational Command of both parts, but absolved from being the administrative authority of either.

So, a new Force, called "Force G", was carved out of "Force J". Each part was made a Flag Officer's Command with a staff similar to the one which I had turned over to Sir Philip, and which he retained. I did not doubt that this was more efficient and a more agreeable arrangement, and it was rendered essential by Vian's reluctance to delegate – a reluctance shared to this day by so many Admirals, Generals, and Civil Servants. But it is expensive for the Taxpayer. In this one case it meant that a Force which had been formed, commanded and trained by one Junior Flag Officer with a small staff, was eventually commanded by one senior and two junior Flag Officers, whose combined staffs were three times as big.

I cannot pretend that I was not disappointed at having to leave Combined Operations [to be given command of the Fiji-class cruiser HMS *Jamaica*] just at the moment when victory and fame were ripe for the plucking, but the traditional dislike of the Navy for startling promotion "out of turn" made it inevitable. Yet I have never regretted my two-year interlude with Combined Operations, and I have always been grateful to Mountbatten for having asked me on his staff and the trust which he reposed in me. Mountbatten's service to the Nation, and indeed to the whole Allied cause, have never been sufficiently realised by the public, although they were fully recognised by Winston and by the King. Not so by the Navy.

It is strange to reflect that after serving nearly two years as an Acting Vice Marshal, and for over one year as a full Admiral and Supreme Commander, having paved the way for the liberation of France, and having re-conquered Burma, he only gained about one year's extra seniority at the end of the war. I will say quite bluntly that this was largely due to jealousy. Mountbatten's strength did not lie in exceptional intellectual powers, although he had a clear brain, especially in the field of technical detail with which too many senior Officers cannot be bothered. He also had a flair for diplomacy, and an ability to see where compromise was possible and desirable. But his real power came from an ability to arouse enthusiasm in his subordinates, and this in turn stemmed from the fact that he could think dynamically; that is to say he was able to translate his thoughts into action.

This is where Civil Servants and modern Staff Officers so often fail. This is what so often leads to prolonged inaction. "Masters of Negation" was the phrase often used by Mr Churchill to describe this type of person.

Nothing illustrates the point I am trying to make better than the controversy that has followed the Dieppe raid. Many people believe that because the risk was so great, because the supporting fire which was made available fell so far short of what Mountbatten himself and the Force Commanders had asked for, the operation should never have been carried out. Very well, consider the consequences had negation prevailed, because they are fairly easy to assess. Without the experience of the raid, no firm plans for the invasion would have emerged in 1943, and the American advocates of giving priority to the Far Eastern campaign would have had their way.

Yet this would not have greatly shortened the war with Japan, although it might perhaps have advanced her surrender to the end of 1944. Meanwhile in Europe we should have been committed to Mr Churchill's dream of making the Italian campaign our main effort. Almost certainly this would have allowed the glory and the prize of encompassing the defeat of Germany to go to Russia, and to Russia alone. My guess is that the Rhine today would be the Russian frontier, and the Scandinavian countries would be Russia's satellites.

In short, I hold that the supreme contribution made by men like Mountbatten, and for that matter by men like Mr Churchill himself, is that they were willing to stake their reputations and their careers on the desperate hazards of battles for which there was no true precedents, and from which their advisors often shrank.

Appendix

LETTER FROM WINSTON CHURCHILL

10 Downing Street,
Whitehall.

September, 19, 1954.

My dear Hallett,

The distinguished services you have rendered the country as a naval officer are well known. I am sure that you will prove an admirable successor in the representation of East Croydon to my old colleague, Sir Herbert Williams, who was for so long a prominent Member of the House of Commons.

It is nearly three years since the General Election. No one who looks back to October, 1951, can be blind to the solid achievements of the Conservative Government. First and foremost, we have upheld the prestige of Britain, and today our country holds an influence in world affairs which is exercised powerfully and unremittingly in the cause of peace. Mr Eden's vigour and initiative commands the respect and inspires the hopes of many nations in the Free World.

In the domestic field the Government's policies have put new heart into industry and helped to establish a real prosperity which does not rest on foreign aid but springs from unfettered British enterprise and sparkling skill. We can do a lot, if we are given a fair chance. Progress is obvious. Sterling is once again a currency in which the world has confidence. We are solvent. Our people are producing more, earning more, spending more, and saving more. We are eating more food, better food, and food of our own choice. Employment was never at a higher level in peacetime. Our burdensome taxation has been reduced while at the same time social benefits have been increased. This double process must go on.

Your opponents will no doubt try to win votes on the ground that the cost of living has not yet been stabilised. It is true that some prices have risen, but others have fallen, and the position has been far steadier than it was – or would again be – under the Socialists. Prices have risen less than wage rates and earnings, and the general standard of living has visibly improved.

Further help will be given to pensioners in the light of expert reviews now going forward. We are resolved to make good in full the fall in the value of pensions which they suffered in the years of Socialist inflation.

A word about the new Rent Act, which a Socialist orator recently described as "deliberately designed to reduce the workers' standard of living". That shameful suggestion has a little truth in it as the "war-monger" lie which disgraced the Socialist's campaign at the General Election. The sole object of the Rent Act is to enable the owners to spend money on repairing houses to prevent them falling into decay. It is the tenants who will reap the direct benefit. How improvident it would be to build new homes at the rate of over 300,000 a year as we are doing, if at the same time we left existing houses to degenerate, through neglect, into slums.

The electors of the East Croydon Division are, I am sure, too shrewd to be led astray by electioneering taradiddles. I ask them to give you a majority which will proclaim to the world their continued confidence in the Conservative Government's handling of the nation's affairs.

Yours sincerely,
Winston S. Churchill

Vice Admiral John H. Hallett, C.B. D.S.O.

INDEX